SPINNIN' THE BAR

Brendan McCann

Published by New Generation Publishing in 2019

ISBN: 978-1-78955-584-4

www.newgeneration-publishing.com

New Generation Publishing

Dedicated to my grandchildren,
Ryan Patrick Jackson and Karagh Marie Jackson

My gratitude to my late brother, Tony,
who gave me loyal support,
right up to the end.

Photograph

By April Rooney:

Enniskillen, Co. Fermanagh, N. Ireland.

Contents

Nearly True Stories

(Names have been changed to protect the guilty)

Best Laid Plans

It was Hong Kong 1972. Waldo was making his name as a drummer in the pipe band and was a bit of a rogue in his regiment. Part of the drummer's duties was to learn to play the bugle. No mean task, especially if you were not a natural blower, if you know what I mean.

As hard as Waldo tried, there was one bugle call that absolutely plagued him. None other than the **Last Post**. It was without doubt the most demanding call in any drummer's repertoire!

Plus, there was the fact that when it was played in barracks it was played at **2200hrs** beside the flagpole, quite a distance away but in full view of those on parade at the guardroom. These would include those under routine punishment, the duty sergeant and the duty officer, with the whole ceremony enhanced by the very bright spotlight making the duty drummer stand out like the star in a **West End Show!**

There would also be other personnel who would turn out to watch the ceremony from a distance, such was the allure of the whole occasion.

Now, Waldo had passed the necessary practical tests in front of the **drum major**, who assured Waldo that he was ready to take to the big stage after completing a dry run through with the top bugler at the time. When the big night came Waldo became extremely nervous and decided to have a wee drink to settle his nerves. After three or four drinks Waldo's mates had convinced him that he may not be up to the task! With this in mind a most devious plan was hatched.

This particular plan had been tried and tested several times before and Waldo was assured that it would work. Among Waldo's mates was Billy, who was the bugler at the time of Waldo's dry run through so Waldo trusted him implicitly! The plan was as follows:

Waldo would turn up in his regalia just before 2200hrs and take up his position at the flagpole. For a mere **10 Hong Kong Dollars**, Billy, with bugle in hand, would turn up behind the high hedge immediately behind the flagpole. There he would remain out of sight but could still see Waldo up close and personal and, on the agreed nod from Waldo, Billy would play the call while Waldo went through the motions! Waldo agreed and went off for a few final rehearsals, to convince himself that it would all be all right on the night. As you can see, these boys were doing this a long time before **X Factor** came on the scene!

It had worked for Billy on at least three occasions before and, as far as he was concerned, it would work again this time! Things began to go wrong when Waldo paid Billy up front. A pint in barracks was **80 cents** so, needless to say, on top of what Billy had already drunk the **Ten Dollars** pushed him well over the edge.

Now, unknown to Waldo, this was when the second most devious plan was hatched! The plan was as follows:

Billy recruited one of the most recent but experienced guys posted out to Hong Kong called Wee Albert, who could play all the calls, and for **Five Dollars** would take Billy's place behind the hedge and carry out the original devious plan! It couldn't have been simpler so Billy and Albert celebrated their new found friendship with a couple of wee ones and both rubbed their hands for many other ventures in the future!

Anyway, just before 2200hrs came around, Waldo was in position, having checked that Billy was in position, which was confirmed by a grunt from behind the hedge. Waldo could see everyone on parade outside the guardroom: the normal extra spectators and even some people who were attending a dinner party in honour of a visiting **VIP** came out of the **officers' mess!**

"Holy f**k," Waldo thought to himself. "Please, please God, make this work!"

Waldo placed the bugle up to his mouth and gently placed the mouthpiece to his lips, preparing himself for the greatest con he had ever been involved in accompanied by a breathtaking bugle call.

Then the **shit** hit the fan. As Waldo nodded his head and began to perform the well-rehearsed **mime act**, the music sounded from behind the hedge. Yes folks, it was the hair-raising sound of the **bagpipes!**

Waldo's jaw dropped, the duty **sergeant's** jaw dropped, the duty **officer's** jaw dropped, the remainder of the parade at the guardroom were in a state of convulsions! Tears began to form in Waldo's eyes and **shite** began to form in his boxers! "Holy f**k," said Waldo under his breath.

The **VIP** at the **officers' mess** was heard to comment in a deep southern **American** drawl: "Gee, how do you get your bugles to sound so sweet?"

That was the last time mixing and matching was ever considered by Waldo, Billy and Wee Albert!

It Seemed Like a Good Idea at the Time

Barney and Jimmy were on duty as members of the **barrack guard** in **Hong Kong**. At about half past midnight on a Saturday night/Sunday morning they were on patrol, which included the perimeter and car park of the **sergeants' mess**. The car park was empty except for a minibus waiting to take the last of the usual Saturday night revellers home to the married quarters.

Barney and Jimmy checked the back door of the **mess** and found it to be unlocked. They both nodded to each other and proceeded to investigate further. On going inside they realised they were in the kitchen, which was in darkness apart from a small security light in the ceiling. Making sure they kept very quiet, they decided to snoop around for a bit, just in case they came across anything that they could eat or drink! Or, even a bottle of hooch **(spirits)**, that they could commandeer for suitable refreshment later!

Barney spotted a huge white fridge in the corner and carefully opened the door. Jimmy then began waving his hands and, in a loud whisper of panic, stated the obvious! That the light in the fridge would be seen by anyone passing the large window beside the sink on their way to the car park and the waiting minibus! Barney closed the door slightly and signalled Jimmy to join him and take a look inside the fridge.

Jimmy glanced over his shoulder and out of the window and then … slowly moved across the tiled floor, ensuring he did not bump into anything and make any noise. Barney once again opened the fridge door so as they could both get a good look inside. They both glanced and smiled at each other in unison at the apparition-like scene before them. The **f****n' fridge** was full, from top to bottom, with bottles of white wine!

F**n' gleamin'!** They quickly removed two bottles, shut the fridge door, found two chairs and sat in a dark corner, where they could see through the window and into the car park. They unslung their SLRs (self-loading rifles) and laid them gently on the floor. Then, with smiles like the cat that got the cream, they settled down to drink the wine. **But**, they hadn't realised that they needed something to get the corks out of the bottles!

Barney to the rescue … for he noticed a small kitchen knife on the table next to them and with that he sunk the corks of both bottles of wine, far enough to allow the wine to rise up to the top of the bottle and then, to the delight of the two mates, to be guzzled at their leisure!

Halfway down the bottles they heard voices coming from the car park. Barney jumped up and pushed the back door tight shut! The two mates then crouched in the darkest corner they could find so they wouldn't be seen or discovered if anyone decided to check the back door!

"Well done, Barney!" thought Jimmy.

They both gave a sigh of relief as the minibus and its passengers drove off into the night.

Now then … they couldn't believe their luck. They gave a quick check call on the radio to say all was well, mentioning that they had kept an eye on the car park of the **sergeants' mess** and the last to leave were on their way home! **The guard commander** gave them a "Well done …

and keep up the good work!"

They couldn't help but chuckle and decided not just to finish the bottles they already had but that they would have time for a least one more each.

In no time at all the two mates were laughing and shushing ... and giggling and shushing ... and then just shushing. Tears were streaming down both faces as they slugged the wine!

They got a check call on the radio from the **guard room**, which calmed them down immediately. Barney answered in the usual military style and the minor panic was over! It was time to put the four empty wine bottles in the bin and return to the **guard room**. Making sure there was no evidence of their misdeeds, they turned the handle of the back door ... nothing happened ... tried again ... still nothing happened ... It didn't **f****n' open!**

The two mates looked at each other and mouthed ... "Ooh f**k!" No matter how hard they turned the handle, this way and that way, it still didn't **f****n' open!**

They decided the door must be self-locking and had initially malfunctioned, allowing them into the **mess**, but when they shut it tight later to avoid detection, the lock engaged properly, locking them in the kitchen.

They decided to climb out the large window beside the sink but, when they released the catches to unlock the two side windows, they found that the space that was created was too small for either of them to escape, even when they took off their belts and pouches!

Time was running out, as they had only about twenty minutes to finish their two-hour patrol before returning to the guard room. They put their belt and pouches back on, re-slung their SLRs and made their way to a door at the other end of the kitchen.

Barney turned the handle very, very slowly and began to open the door very, very slowly. It led into a dimly lit hot plate and dining room area. The two mates tiptoed towards another door, which led to a dimly lit hallway.

Suddenly, they heard several voices, and then the clink of glasses, and then the sound of giggles, and then all the voices were drowned out with whoops of laughter!

Barney and Jimmy began to shake with panic, when they noticed another door at the end of the hallway. They immediately **sprint tiptoed** along the hallway and turned the handle gingerly. As the door opened and the hot humid night air hit their sweat ridden faces, a smile of relief came over both of them.

Just before Barney closed the door he heard someone shout: “Another round on mess guests!”

Barney wondered what that meant but found out a few years later: **Much to his delight! (Hee hee hee)**.

Don't Judge a Book by its Cover

Richie and Cecil were in **Singapore** for a few days off prior to returning to the UK. They were sharing a twin room in a nice hotel, a short distance from the city centre. The first day saw them visit the normal sightseeing locations but, late into the afternoon, they decided to visit some of the bars near their hotel. They met many other revellers and soon the few drinks before dinner turned into a bit of a sing-song and party with everyone (old friends and new) joining in with the singing and the dancing!

After numerous drinks, one of the new friends suggested going to an even better bar not too far away, in a street called **Boogie Street**. So, Ritchie and Cecil agreed that it sounded like a good idea and off they went with their new-found friend to carry on the movement, with the chance of a few **Dolly Birds** thrown in!

When they arrived in **Boogie Street**, every bar seemed to be having a hell of a party and every bar was crammed with good-looking women! Ritchie and Cecil were brought to one particular bar, where their new-found friend, was well known and, lo and behold, the party took off at a rate of knots that was bordering on **debauchery!**

Ritchie and Cecil soon got acquainted with numerous women, all of whom were **drop dead gorgeous** and all of whom were definitely **up for it!**

Swapping of **spit** and the groping of **tits** and **cocks** were high on the agenda, and dancing to the music, played on the thunderously loud jukebox referred to as **crutch grinding music or the erection selection!**

Ritchie and Cecil were becoming very familiar with two **blonde bombshells** from **Australia**, who had fantastic suntans, schoolgirl tits and unbelievable legs, covered very slightly with very tight sexy miniskirts that left little to the imagination. The two mates were going weak at the knees.

When the two **blonde bombshells** suggested that all four of them should head back to the boys' hotel, Ritchie and Cecil hailed a taxi **PDQ!**

All four of them piled into the back seat of the taxi, to carry on with the groping and the slobbering until they reached their destination.

On arrival at the hotel, it wasn't long until they paired off, having already changed partners in the bar and then in the taxi. Ritchie and Cecil found themselves in their beds, each with a **blonde bombshell** in their arms! **What Bliss!**

After about five or ten minutes, Cecil shouted out: "Ritchie! Ritchie! My one's got a pair of bollix!"

To which Ritchie replied: "Ah Cecil, any port in a f****n' storm!"

The Life and Times of Mark Blackburn

1. Don't Take Your Eye Off the Ball

Mark was a pipe band side drummer serving in a well-known Army regiment. He had a great personality, a great sense of humour and was definitely a ladies' man. He sometimes found himself in a pickle that wasn't always his own doing, although some would say that it was poetic justice!

On completion of the Queen's Guard mount in London, the pipe band formed up in two ranks to march back to barracks. No music was required for this journey, so the pipes were put safely away under each piper's left arm and each side drummer slung his drum to the side. The top of the drum was facing in and against the left leg, with the bottom of the drum facing outwards.

Attached to the bottom of each side drum were two white knotted ropes known as drag ropes. These were for ornamental purposes only, dating back many years in history when they were actually used to tighten the rims, which were situated on the top and bottom of each drum. **(Before screw tension drums were introduced to the British Army)**.

Historically, the drag ropes were also used to carry the drum on the drummer's back, a drag rope over each shoulder, and carried similar to that of a backpack.

On marching up **The Mall** (the main road leading from St James's Palace, past Buckingham Palace and onwards to Wellington Barracks) with the pipe major in line with the last two drummers, **(maintaining control of the pipe**

band), various vehicles were slowing down to enable the tourists within to lean out of the windows to capture a close-up photograph of the individuals.

On most occasions, by the time the tourists had zoomed in for the prize photo, the side drummers at the rear were the subject of the close-ups and personal adoration! But, as they say, **there's always f****n' one!**

One of the famous **(or infamous)**, London cabs travelling in the opposite direction, actually crossed **The Mall!** Thus, it met the pipe band almost head-on and stopped abruptly!

The pipe major ordered the leading two pipers to march around to the right of the London cab, taking the remainder of the band with them, to hopefully avoid an unfortunate situation or confrontation.

Two blonde American honeys stretched out of the window nearest to the band and screamed: "Smile for us, ya all."

Then it was flash, bang, wallop! Big cheesy smiles by the Yanks and by certain members of the band, with the pipe major cursing and swearing, making unmentionable threats under his breath directed at anyone within range!

Out of the blue, a mounted London policeman arrived and, very quickly, the driver of the London cab pulled off. At the same time, Mark moved so close to the cab to get a closer look at the busty Yanks, the unbelievable happened.

As the cab pulled off, Mark's drag ropes became entangled with the rear bumper of the vehicle and off he went, about five miles an hour, backwards! To which the pipe major yelled: "Blackburn, get f****n' back here!"

Fortunately, the cab driver had spotted immediately what happened and hit the brakes, which resulted in Mark almost doing a back flip, but somehow managing to stay on his feet, keep hold of the side drum and, above all else, keep his bearskin just about on his head.

The cab driver took off with the two busty Yanks, who continued their never-to-be-repeated photo session. The pipe major was threatening to put Mark in jail, with the remainder of the band looking to their front but just **f****n' dyin'** to glance over their shoulders.

Mark had an idea the next day: he thought about getting a few days off by reporting sick **with whiplash!**

* * *

2. It Never Rains but it Pours

Mark once again was on parade with the pipe band, this time at Windsor Castle. The guard mount had been successfully completed, with the pipe band playing some great marching tunes through the streets of Windsor with the dismounting guard, known as the Old Guard, marching smartly behind.

Due to several showers of rain earlier that morning, there were a few puddles here and there throughout their route back to barracks, but this did not deter those on parade from showing off their musical and marching skills for the tourists and the local Windsorians.

The side drum sling carries the side drum with the aid of a brass ring at the bottom of the sling. This in turn is engaged to the side drum hook, which in turn is situated on the top rim of the said side drum.

Anyway, there's good ol' Mark playing away, showing off as usual, smiling and winking his eye at anything in a skirt or out of a skirt for that matter when, once again, the unbelievable happened.

Mark's brass ring, at the bottom of his side drum sling, disengaged itself from its position, allowing the weight of the side drum to carry it in a downwards direction and bounce several times, before coming to an abrupt stop, a few yards in front of him!

Mark quickly bent over to retrieve the side drum. At this point, his bearskin toppled from his head and fell into a puddle of rainwater in front of the side drum!

Mark was beginning to lose ground on the remainder of the pipe band but the Old Guard, marching immediately behind, was gaining ground.

The supervising warrant officer of the Old Guard quickly gave the word of command: **mark time**!

And then quickly added: **Blackburn! Pick up that f****n' drum, before I shove it up your f****n' arse**!

Within a split second, the side drum was in Mark's arms and his bearskin firmly back on his poor unfortunate head! He was confined to barracks for seven days and was lucky not to also receive a hefty fine!

But hey, there wasn't a dry eye in the house!

* * *

3. Teething Problems

Mark also played the guitar and sang in a wee Irish band in his spare time. Most of that spare time, especially at weekends, was spent earning extra money playing in various bars in north London.

Now, most of the customers were hard-working and hard-drinking Irish builders and there was always a bit of spare available **(loose women!)**. Mark loved to show off to any young, or not so young ladies who may have taken a fancy to him and he was always up for a bit of skulduggery!

Mark asked his good friend and fellow chancer, Barney, to come with him one Saturday night to watch the wee Irish band and have a few jars with a promise that they would both definitely get lucky with some of the female customers! Barney jumped at the chance and both arrived at the venue in north London for, hopefully, a great party night!

As the band played through their first set, requests were made for some of the local talent to strut their stuff during the band's second set, which of course added to the party atmosphere. Barney also took part on the drum kit as he was also a drummer with Mark in the same well-known pipe band!

After hearing Barney on the drums, some of the local girls began making themselves readily available at the bar and most of them weren't backward about being forward!

Some of the diehard Paddies were also offering to buy Barney a drink! Mark was getting just a wee bit upset as Barney was getting all the spoils of the night.

Now, in between songs towards the end of the band's second set, Mark signalled for Barney to approach the stage and instructed him in a devilish plan to make some extra money.

Barney returned to the bar where the groupies had begun to gather, and by this time about six or seven of the Irish builders were also in attendance.

Barney then made an important announcement to the crowd that had gathered close to him: "I'll bet any man here a £1, that Mark can play his guitar with his teeth!"

A cheer went up and about fifteen men and women put **£1** notes into a pint glass and Barney agreed to cover all bets **(A lot of money in 1974)**.

A few minutes later, the wee Irish band broke into a **rock 'n' roll jig** and the whole place went **f****n' mad** with dancin' and clappin' their hands!

Barney then shouts: "Right Mark! Play the guitar with yer teeth!"

Mark nodded and then proceeded to take out his top four front false teeth.

With a toothless grin and fangs each side of the gaping hole at the front of his mouth, Mark, with the aid of his dentures held in his right hand, played his guitar like a **f****n' lunatic**!

Barney then realised that his whole world was about to come to an end when he grabbed the pint glass full of the betting money and ran out the door.

As luck would have it, there was a taxi rank about a hundred yards up the main road he now found himself sprinting along, still grasping the glass with the money!

He could hear the screams and howls of those he had left behind and then he heard the dreaded sound of footsteps behind him: getting closer and closer and f****n' closer!

Barney didn't dare look back. He just ran as fast as he could, got to the taxi, opened the door, jumped in, and was about to close the door when a hand appeared on the door handle!

Barney was ready to stick the boot in when a familiar face appeared in the doorway of the taxi: **It was f****n' Mark!**

Around his neck was strapped his guitar and he was panting like a mad dog on heat. Very quick and very loud instructions were given to the taxi driver, with the promise of a very large tip, and off they went at a very high speed!

On their journey to safety, Barney, on several occasions, tried to strangle Mark with his guitar strap!

The guitar was only slightly damaged, and Mark finally agreed that Barney should get the lion's share of their ill-gotten gains. It has to be said that a rematch at that pub in north London **never, ever, materialised!**

Oops, Sorry

Tony and Jimmy were having a great time in the mess at happy hour on a Friday afternoon. After a couple of hours they decided to go down to the local pub for a change of scenery. When they arrived, Tony paid for two pints of lager for himself and Jimmy. He also paid for a packet of cheese and onion crisps.

The pub was quite quiet so they phoned for a taxi, to take them to another pub that would be livelier. There would be about a twenty-minute wait, just time to finish the drinks and get another one each.

While they were waiting, a crowd of Irish builders came in from a building site opposite the pub, for a well-earned, end of week drink. Tony decided to go to the gents before the taxi arrived. When he returned to the bar, where Jimmy was still drinking his pint, there was a huge Irish builder eating the packet of cheese and onion crisps that Tony had left on the bar!

Tony and Jimmy looked at each other and noticed that the remainder of the **big fella's** mates were scattered around the pub drinking at a speed that would put **Niagara Falls** to shame! Beside the **big fella** was a pint of **Guinness** and a **very large whiskey**.

So, Tony decides it's time for a spot of retaliation and winks at Jimmy. At this point Jimmy hasn't a clue what Tony had in mind and is very worried about the outcome, to say the least.

Tony picks up the packet of crisps, takes a mouthful and **bangs** the packet down on the bar, between the pint of Guinness and the pint of lager. **(As if to say, "f**k you!")**.

The **big fella** looks at Tony, waits for a few seconds and he then does exactly the same!

This sequence of events occurred a further two times, with the amount of crisps being eaten increasing in volume on each occasion. Jimmy's whole life is now flashing through his mind, and he's praying that the taxi turns up pretty soon.

The **big fella** goes to the gents. The taxi turns up outside. Tony drinks the **big fella's very large whiskey**, and he and Jimmy run like blazes for the taxi, laughing all the way to the next pub.

When they arrived Tony ordered two pints, still laughing …

He then put his hand into his overcoat pocket to get his cigarettes and took out **a packet of cheese and onion crisps!**

Sunshine Surprise

Mark was in **Cyprus** training with his unit. When not required for duty, he would take advantage of any free time and, with his boozing buddies, go into **Limassol** for a few beers, a bite to eat and maybe sample some of the delights on offer from some of the female tourists, who were also looking for a good time with no strings attached!

On one occasion, Mark and his mates met up with a group of girls from England and, after the usual banter and chatting up, they all made their way to a disco in town, not too far from the girls' accommodation. **("Good idea," thought Mark)**.

Drinks were flowing, dancing was hectic to say the least and Mark realised that he was, in fact, strutting his stuff better than anyone else in the disco. Even Lucy, the girl he was trying to impress, had difficulty keeping up with him! Mark thought he would give her a rest at the end of the current record, as she appeared to be limping slightly **(Maybe she pulled a muscle or something)**.

Anyway, Mark and Lucy made their way to a secluded booth with a candlelit table and soon began to chew the face off each other. Now, Lucy was quite a good looker, not the usual **dog breath** with which Mark had become used to.

She also looked very sexy with her skimpy top, giving a great view of her **sun-tanned cleavage**, and a pair of skin tight jeans that showed off an **arse** you would die for! Mark thought that **Christmas** had come early, especially when Lucy suggested they go back to her room. The girl she shared with was still having a great time on the dance floor.

So, off they went, Lucy staggering slightly but Mark being the perfect gentleman, for the time being anyway, and he assisted her every so often when Lucy seemed to lose her balance.

Mark made sure he put his hands in all the right places to ensure that the eggs would be delivered without any cracks! After some time, they arrived at Lucy's holiday villa and Mark thought that this could well be the night that all his dreams would come true!

His eyes nearly popped out of their sockets when he saw the **f****n' swimming pool!** His mind raced from sex in the pool, to three in a bed, to riding like the winner of the **Grand National!**

When they arrived at Lucy's room, she suggested that they share a shower to help them to cool down a bit! Mark thought: "There really is a GOD!!"

Anyway, Mark couldn't get his clothes off quick enough and, after staggering around the room, he eventually fell in a heap laughing. Now, Lucy was also staggering or stumbling or whatever but she managed to get to the shower first, which dented Mark's pride, just a wee bit.

He soon remedied the situation and, with his **manhood** at the **gallop**, he sauntered into the bathroom, pulled back the shower curtain and there she was: **just waiting for it!**

Mark first noticed her beautiful **tits** and then, as his eyes moved slowly downwards past her well-trimmed **minge**, he noticed something he hadn't noticed before: **Lucy had the bottom half of her left leg missing!**

Thus, the reason for Lucy's unsteadiness throughout the night, she had a prosthetic limb! Mark rose to the challenge and gave her a good seeing to right there in the shower! When, after the event, he was asked how he managed to keep her balanced while he carried out the dirty deed, he answered: "Sure, I just stuck her stump in the f****n' soap dish!"

Ah but, the story doesn't end there because Mark saw Lucy again on another booze-filled night and this time they made use of the swimming pool. When asked how that particular date went he answered: "Sure, she kept swimmin' round in f****n' circles!"

Seven into One

Harvey, Charlie and Barney, Trigger and Ignatius were having a drink in the bar with two nurses who worked in the local hospital: Milly from Ireland and Molly from Scotland.

The girls had hourglass figures and pretty faces. Both had jet black, shoulder length hair and both were wearing revealing V-neck tops, finished off with sexy miniskirts.

The drinks were flowing well with the boys on pints of **lager**, Molly on **Bacardi and Coke** and Milly on pints of **Guinness!**

Now, at this point it has to be said that the boys were having trouble keeping up with Milly, with Molly thanking **God** that she was on the shorts! As the night wore on Harvey was swapping spit with Milly and Charlie was doing likewise with Molly. Trigger, Barney and Ignatius were taking advantage of the lull in the battle to catch up with Milly on the pints.

At about half past nine, Milly mentioned that the nightclub, called **Bunter's**, in the local town had drinks at half price due to a special midweek promotion. The deadline for the £5 entry fee was 10pm … thereafter it would cost £10!

So, a quick nod from everyone there and Ignatius, being the only one with a car, was unanimously voted as the duty driver. Ignatius would, in fact, squeeze us all into his two-door **red Hillman Imp**. We all agreed that he would have his £5 entry fee paid, he would not have to buy any rounds for the remainder of the night and Trigger and Barney would pay for the taxi home! The other four would make their own arrangements.

Ignatius reluctantly agreed and all seven of them made their way to the car park to the waiting transport, with Barney suggesting who should sit where in what can only be described as a tight squeeze!

Now, Barney was of sound mind to realise that the best seat apart from the driver's was the front passenger's seat, so, with that in mind and reminding Ignatius that he was getting a free taxi home, the other five were placed into the back seat as follows: in behind the driver was Harvey with Milly on his knee. In the middle would be Trigger, because he was so skinny. In behind Barney would be Charlie with Molly on his knee. With the journey only going to take about 15 minutes, sure, who could complain!

Off they went to **Bunter's** with Harvey and Charlie ramming their tongues down their respective woman's throat. Trigger was moaning because he felt like a **sardine** between the two grappling couples. Ignatius was saying the **Our Father** because the car, due to being overloaded, was swaying all over the road and he didn't want to meet his maker **just yet!**

Barney was sitting there trying not to laugh, being so glad that everyone had accepted his plan of action and couldn't change it now as they were nearly halfway there.

Throughout the journey, Barney glanced over his right shoulder to check if everyone was all right, assuring them that they would soon be at **Bunter's**.

He noticed that, although Harvey was still swapping spit with Milly, unfortunately for Harvey, Milly kept pulling away from him, and there wasn't much room with Trigger stuck in the middle. It was becoming more like a **Carry**

On film with arms, legs, heads, tongues and many other parts of the anatomy almost in ***Full Flight!***

At this stage, Harvey was beginning to lose the rag and began **cursin'** *and* **swearin'**, with Milly getting more and more upset. The more she tried to pull away, the more Harvey tried to pull her closer, with **slobbers** beginning to form all around his mouth, dribbling down and off the end of his chin! Then, as they pulled up outside **Bunter's**, it all **HAPPENED!**

Milly pulled away from Harvey once more and up it came, from the soles of her feet: **warm f****n' Guinness!**

Just as Harvey was going in with his tongue one last time, the **warm Guinness** hit him on the roof of his mouth! He in turn puked over Trigger, who could see what was coming but couldn't move a bloody inch.

Trigger, in turn, puked over Charlie and Molly, with Charlie puking over Molly's bare tits and Molly, the dirty rotten filthy bitch, puking all over the back of Barney's **f****n' head!** The inside of the **Hillman Imp** was now swimming in **vomit!**

Ignatius, the only one of them not to succumb to the **vomit**, quickly jumped out and was screaming **blue bloody murder!** The remainder of us piled out as fast as the arms, legs and **vomit** would allow.

Thankfully, there were toilets just to the right of the main foyer of the club and, as the gang of five from the back of the car made their way there to sort themselves out, Ignatius and Barney stood in disbelief about what had just happened to them.

In the end, they got some paper towels from the club toilets, cleaned out the car as best as possible, and Barney then suggested leaving the windows down overnight and collecting the car sometime the following day.

To which Ignatius screamed: "Some bastard might steal me car!"

To which Barney screamed even louder: "In the name of F**K, who in their right mind, is gonna steal that stinkin' heap o' SHITE?"

Never Send a Boy to do a Man's Job

Paddy and Barney were instructors together at an Army recruit depot in southern England. Barney was training the adult recruits and Paddy was training the juniors (15 to 17-year-olds).

They would both run into each other on a daily basis or in the mess for social events. On one occasion Barney decided to walk from his office the 300 yards to Paddy's office to cadge a cigarette and a wee cup of tea.

It was about 7pm and as they were both working late, a well-deserved break was in order as all those under training had finished their evening meal and were engaged in that well-known pastime: **shining parade!**

Barney and Paddy would quite often have friendly banter regarding the mentality of some of the dickheads they were training, and the frequent, ridiculous situations into which they got themselves.

Now, when Paddy and Barney settled down to their wee cups of tea, which in fact were huge great black plastic mugs, they discovered to their horror that they both had run out of fags! Paddy immediately screamed for one of his juniors to present himself: **PDQ!**

Paddy tells Barney that this in fact, is one of his best men. Barney is quick to remind Paddy that his best man is a mere boy. Paddy disguises the fact that he has taken minor offence to this outrageous remark and proceeds to give the terrified young lad, the following instructions: "Right ney. You go down to the NAAFI shop and get me twenty Embassy cigarettes. Here's the money. Be as fast as yer wee legs will carry ya. I want ya back here ASAP! Or even quicker! And if they haven't got Embassy, just get anything. Do ya understand me ney?"

The young lad nodded furiously and proceeded to make his way out of the office like a headless chicken!

About fifteen minutes later the young lad appeared back at Paddy's office, sweating like a whore in a **gang bang!**

Paddy reached out for the Embassy cigarettes with an anticipating smile of satisfaction on his face, when, to his horror, his best man produced a brown, paper bag, from behind his back.

Paddy: "What's in the bag?"

Young Lad: "Well … they didn't have any Embassy cigarettes, Sergeant … and … and … You said: 'Just get anything'."

Paddy screams: "Well then, what did ya get me?"

The reply came loud and sure: "A lovely pork pie, Sergeant!"

Paddy screams again: "A f****n' lovely pork pie?"

Young Lad: "Yes Sergeant! They were on special offer … and … and … you said: 'Just get anything'."

At this stage Barney is in bits under Paddy's desk. However, he looked up in time to see the young lad sprinting out through the door with the lovely pork pie now firmly attached to the top of his forehead.

Paddy's complexion was completely purple and Barney said: "Yer best f****n' man; my f****n' arse!"

The life and times of Jimmy McGill

1. Follow Through

Jimmy was on three weeks' summer leave from his unit in London. His home town of Glasgow was always a great place to party and tell wondrous tales of his escapades, so he couldn't get there quickly enough! Unlike many occasions in the past, he picked up a bit of part-time work in a bar in the centre of town so he wasn't his usual skint self as his return date approached.

On his last day of leave he was financially secure to the point he painted the town red with a few old mates and dallied with a few grateful women, who were more than willing to show their appreciation to this man of the world.

Day turned into night, then into the wee small hours, then into morning when he finally fell asleep, cuddling a huge fish supper along with two equally huge saveloy sausages! All covered in HP sauce and plenty of salt and vinegar!

When he awoke at about eleven o'clock that morning, with his head bouncing and with hunger clawing at his alcohol-filled belly, he smiled as he realised he had not yet eaten the previous night's feast! Bang! Flash! Wallop! The cold stale food was gone in less than ten minutes!

He checked his wristwatch and determined he had enough time for a few more pints before getting the train back to London at three o'clock that afternoon.

However, he had a small problem. All his kit, although packed and ready to go, was at his mother's house at the other side of town. His mother would be at work and, since Jimmy had said his goodbyes to her the day before, she wouldn't mind if Jimmy asked his 15-year-old brother Willie, who was still on school holidays, to bring the said kit into town, where they could meet up.

Whereupon Jimmy would thank his younger brother by treating him to a few sly pints in the pub, where Jimmy had worked part-time during his leave period.

The necessary phone call was made and Jimmy met up with Willie in town. Jimmy's overloaded suitcase, which was bulging at the seams and held closed with the help of two leather belts, was deposited at the left luggage in the train station, which was only a five-minute walk from the pub.

They sat in the side snug away from prying eyes, with the duty barman giving Jimmy and the 15-year-old Willie a wink and a nod whenever Willie was sinking his pint.

At about a quarter to three, goodbyes and handshakes were exchanged, drinks were quickly drained and the two brothers made their way, slightly the worse for wear, in the general direction of the train station.

Jimmy felt a wee bit of an upset in his belly, enhanced by the odd rift and the odd rip-roaring fart!

He thought to himself that having so many pints on top of all that greasy, cold, stale food, with the odd bit of skin from the chips coming away from his back teeth, would possibly lead to an unavoidable predicament.

Then it happened: **the greatest f****n' fart in history!**

And would you believe it: **the greatest f****n' follow through!**

They were only a stone's throw away from the train station and Jimmy stank to high heaven!

He leaned against a nearby shop window hoping no one would notice the seriousness of his plight, when he noticed a branch of Marks and Spencer across the street.

As his arse began to stick to his underpants, and the slight trickle of liquid began to make its way down under his crutch, he whispered to Willie to go across the street to Marks and Spencer and buy a pair of 38 regular denims: **and f****n' hurry up!**

Armed with the handful of notes that were shoved into his hand, Willie ran to the department store, almost getting run down by a speeding bus, and returned forthwith with the said item, to Jimmy's absolute delight!

They both made their way to the left luggage, quickly retrieving Jimmy's overloaded suitcase, and then, at a severe rate of knots, made their way to the London train platform, where Jimmy said a very quick goodbye to Willie.

The big brother slipped the wee brother a fiver for performing the life-saving task and, above all, not asking his big brother any embarrassing questions!

Immediately on boarding the train, Jimmy found a luggage rack to store his suitcase and made his way to the toilets post haste with the Marks and Spencer bag.

He locked himself in and removed the denims he was wearing plus the diarrhoea-soaked underpants. There was no toilet paper available so, by folding the underpants in two, he managed to find a clean piece of material to wipe his arse! Alas: this was not enough to clean up the mess, especially the trickle that had made its way down the back of his legs!

Jimmy then had a brainwave!

Off came his Chelsea boots, followed by his socks! The socks finished off the clean-up job, no trouble at all. **Ha ha!**

He then waited until the train pulled out of the station and made its way out of Glasgow to ensure that the general area of the city was left behind. He then forced open the dirty, sticky, small window in the toilet and, after a push and a squeeze, all the offending items – underpants, socks and jeans – were catapulted into the local countryside.

Thankfully, his T-shirt had escaped pollution and there he stood with a great big satisfactory smile on his face … naked from the waist down.

Jimmy opened the plastic bag to remove the denim jeans – and withdrew a 38 regular denim … **f****n' jacket!!!**

His whole life flashed before his eyes, as did his most successful Army career! And, to add fuel to the fire the train conductor was banging on the toilet door for a **f****n' ticket check!**

Needless to say, with the help of a very understanding train conductor, Jimmy survived to tell the tale and he also learned a very valuable lesson: Don't trust your wee brother, to get anything f****n' right!!!

* * *

2. Unlikely Misfortunes

Jimmy and his on-off girlfriend Bridget were having a whale of a time in the sergeants' mess on a typical Saturday night session! The food was good, the beer was cool and Bridget was … ***Hot Hot Hot!***

They left the sounds of the disco behind in the wee small hours and made their way to Jimmy's room, which was situated on the third floor of the sergeants' mess accommodation, adjacent to the main building and connected by the corridor on the ground floor.

Now, in those days, it was frowned upon, to say the least, and punishable by the powers that be to allow unauthorised personnel, particularly a civilian female, access to sergeants' mess bedrooms!

However, there were certain occasions when a blind eye and a deaf ear would be applied, depending on the circumstances and the character of the offending individual.

At about six o'clock that morning, Jimmy awoke to find Bridget missing from the room: then he heard her voice saying: "Jimmy, Jimmy. I can't find your f****n' room. Come and get me!"

Jimmy jumped out of bed in his best Y-fronts, pulled them well up over his love handles and gently opened the door. Bridget nearly jumped out of her skin, as she was standing next to that very door.

She was dressed only in Jimmy's green Army issue towel, which was wrapped around the most important places and definitely under pressure from her ample **do wa diddy diddies!**

Jimmy dragged her into the room and asked where she had been. She explained that she needed to pee and, since his room was not en suite, she tried to find the toilets, but unfortunately couldn't find them anywhere so she made her way down to the ground floor, to use the ladies toilets close to the sergeants' mess bar that she had used while they were partying earlier.

"Holy f**k!" said Jimmy. "Did anybody see you?"

With a nonchalant air Bridget replied: "Just a big tall man, with silver hair, who asked who I was and allowed me to go about my business."

Jimmy thought for a moment and then said: "Just a big tall man, with silver hair? Who the F**K could it be? Not to worry, it must be one of my mates. I'm surprised he allowed you to get back in one f****n' piece!"

Anyway, later that Sunday morning, Jimmy slipped on his jeans, a pullover and his best flip-flops and made his way to the dining room on the ground floor next to the bar.

He picked up a pot of tea, milk, toast, a few rashers of bacon, two mugs, and two glasses of orange. He then placed them all on a neat napkin-covered tray and prepared to deliver the goods to Bridget in the room, where he felt sure he would be duly rewarded for his efforts!

As he was making his way from the hotplate through the dining room, there in the doorway stood the boss man in uniform: **Big Bill!** The regimental sergeant major: in all his glory.

Just a big tall man, with silver hair!

Stood next to **Big Bill** was his right hand man: **Willie the Dog!**

Well, Jimmy nearly dropped the overloaded tray. He then began to shake, slightly at first, then almost out of control, not knowing if it was a case of the **hippy hippy shakes** or if he was suffering from shock!

Big Bill looked down at the gibbering wreck that stood before him and said in his infamous, sarcastic, bellowing voice: "Was that your half-naked tart I saw wandering around the corridors first thing this morning, McGill?"

Jimmy swallowed hard, took a deep breath and tried to explain but, unfortunately, all that came out of his mouth was a form of **Scottish Gallic!**

Before he could finish, **Willie the Dog** screamed: "The next time she needs a pish, tell her to use the f****n' sink in your room!"

With that, **Big Bill** and **Willie the Dog** made their way towards the hotplate, allowing Jimmy, still managing not to drop the overloaded tray, to make his escape back to his room and the waiting Bridget: Making sure that he kept the cheeks of his arse clinched tight shut!

Later that afternoon, when the coast was clear, Jimmy and Bridget returned to the bar on the ground floor to top up their intake of alcoholic beverages and relate the incident with **Big Bill** and **Willie the Dog** to the many, unbelieving, fellow party animals.

Afternoon turned into early evening and, with only one thing on his mind, the bold Jimmy whisked Bridget upstairs, for a well-earned further helping of lust-making!

Knowing that Bridget had arranged a lift from her flat mate at midnight, due to the fact she had an early start the following morning, Jimmy decided that an Olympic performance between the sheets was definitely in order.

Jimmy's alarm clock went off at eleven o'clock that night to give Bridget time to sort herself out and slip downstairs for her lift home. Jimmy needed to go to the toilet and, when Bridget explained that she also needed to go, was politely told: "Ah for f**k's sake. Do it in the sink woman!"

Jimmy returned to the room about ten minutes later to find Bridget sitting on the end of the bed putting on her slacks. Then it hit him like a sucker punch.

An unbelievable stench had enveloped the small room: and then he saw it!

A great big turd!!!

It just sat there, curled round the plughole of the sink, and the front and back pages of the *Sun* newspaper that had been used to wipe her arse were scrunched up in the waste paper bin under the desecrated sink!

Jimmy had to control his urge to kick her all around the room and quickly opened the window to help alleviate the lingering aroma, at the same time, cursin' and swearin' but not too loud for fear someone would hear the commotion.

He then turned on both taps of the sink and quickly looked for something, anything, that would help to break the **turd** up into smaller pieces so he could force it down the plughole.

The nearest thing was a spare toothbrush in the glass beside the sink. Quickly he prodded and prodded until he nearly puked up but, in the end, his fighting spirit paid off and the offending object was dispersed.

By this time, Bridget had her head bowed into her hands and was in tears, so Jimmy tried to calm her and himself down.

He decided the next best thing to do was to get rid of the **shitey** newspaper and, without further ado, he took it to the toilets along the corridor to flush it down the lavatory.

When he returned to the room guess what Bridget was doing? Only cleaning her **f****n'** teeth with the same **f****n'** toothbrush that Jimmy had used to clear the **shitey** sink!

Jimmy said nothing as it would just have made matters worse.

A wee while later, they made their way downstairs for the midnight lift. As they were waiting in the dark shadows of the main doorway, Bridget tried very hard to apologise, but Jimmy told her not to worry as he had forgiven her for the misunderstanding with the sink.

She didn't believe him as he kept pulling away every time she tried to give him a good night kiss.

The lift finally arrived and Bridget made one last attempt to console Jimmy. In the end he had to give in and Bridget gave him a long, lingering, sexy, French kiss.

She was no sooner in the car and gone when Jimmy raced up the stairs and drank and gargled almost a half-bottle of Grouse whisky, before falling asleep into an alcohol-fuelled slumber.

Talk about someone leaving a bad taste in your mouth!

The Life and Times of Daz and Gaz

1. Sunny Side UP

Daz and Gaz were stationed in the centre of London. The bright lights of the metropolis were a great pastime, and nights out came at a rapid rate at the beginning of the month. However, towards the end of the month, money was tight to say the least! When the last weekend approached they were normally skint! On one such occasion the cavalry arrived, via a 21st birthday card from Daz's mum with £20 inserted. It wasn't much for a night out, but they decided to go to a bar not too far from barracks called **The Bag O' Nails**, situated on Buckingham Palace Road.

It was a Friday night and the bar was very busy when they arrived at about nine o'clock. There was a lounge bar upstairs where Daz had met a local girl the previous week and he hoped that she might show up again, with the possibility of a second helping of what had been on offer on their first encounter. He and Gaz might even get an invitation back to her flat that she shared with her mate, which was somewhere in Victoria.

At about half past ten, none of the girls had showed up! Thinking that they would be heading back to barracks for an early night and a boring weekend, they decided to spend the last of their money on one for the road.

When Daz was at the bar, Gaz caught the eye of a very well-dressed middle-aged man sitting two tables away, who appeared to be drinking very large gin and tonics. Before Daz had paid for their last two pints, the very well-dressed middle-aged man sauntered up close to him, paid for the two beers, then promptly ordered and paid for another two! The next thing you know, Daz and the well-dressed stranger were heading towards Gaz, talking away as if they were old friends!

The two mates couldn't believe their luck when their new-found friend got another round in, just before eleven o'clock! After a few more minutes of small talk, Daz explained that they were serving soldiers out for a few beers and unfortunately they were financially embarrassed. The well-dressed stranger told them his name. He said in a very polite manner:

"My name is Valentine … Yes, Valentine … Primrose … O'Toole. Everyone calls me VP!"

With that he burst out laughing in a very high-pitched tone! The two mates looked at each other in absolute wonderment, whispering unrepeatable profanities under their breaths! Then **VP** explained his situation and a proposal that sounded dodgy to say the least!

The upcoming weekend was his first weekend off for a very long time and he intended to party right through until Monday morning. However, his long-time male security escort and bodyguard had let him down at the last minute.

VP explained that he was a very wealthy man and required protection when out and about in London, especially when partying! He then offered the two mates a no strings attached deal that would be very profitable for them and equally suitable for him!

They must simply accompany him on his travels over the weekend as his escorts, have free drinks and be handsomely paid for their efforts. The first party was a short taxi ride from the pub and he had planned to go there as soon as the pub had closed, so they needed to make up their minds **PDQ!**

Daz and Gaz didn't need much persuasion, thanks to the free beers that they had nearly finished and the fact that they were just about flat broke! A wink was as good as a nod, and so all three made their way outside and into one of the many taxis available on Buckingham Palace Road.

It wasn't long before they arrived outside a block of apartments somewhere in Chelsea. **VP** paid the taxi driver, including a very handsome tip that did not go unnoticed by Daz and Gaz! In they went to a ground floor apartment that was packed with revellers drinking and dancing. They were greeted by the host, an equally well-dressed middle-aged man who was given a brief update on the situation by **VP**.

Daz and Gaz were instructed that at least one of them had to remain close to **VP** but were encouraged to enjoy themselves. There were definitely more men than women but the drink was flowing and the makeshift disco was blasting out top twenty-style records, beside a well-stocked bar!

Nobody made any moves on **VP** or the two newest escorts throughout the whole time they were there. The happy trio had a fantastic time up until they left by taxi, at about six o'clock the following morning! **VP** insisted Daz and Gaz share a twin room at his mansion in an area known as **Great Hollands** in west London. He also reassured them that there was no hidden agenda!

At about two o'clock that afternoon the two mates were woken by **VP**, who had been busy preparing a lovely lunch of steak, egg and chips. They couldn't believe their luck!

Down went the grub, with the help of large helpings of ice-cold Buck's Fizz! **VP** produced **£100** in £20 notes for the previous night's work by Daz and Gaz and offered the same amount for their services if they would make themselves available for the Saturday night. The two friends didn't need much persuading and agreed immediately.

The Saturday night routine was pretty much the same as Friday night, except they ended up at four different parties in different parts of the west end of London. They were paraded by **VP** everywhere they went, with strict instructions to everyone else: **hands off!**

After another long night and an equally long lie-in on the Sunday at **VP's** mansion, once again the two friends were woken by **VP** with another full plate of steak, egg and chips! Once again **£100** was produced for the previous night's work with, would you believe it, the same offer for Sunday night!

Well, Daz and Gaz jumped at the chance but mentioned that they would need to be away sharpish on Monday morning to return to barracks in time for their first parade. The deal was struck and once again the routine of party after party began, but the two friends insisted they had an alarm clock to waken them on the following morning. Once again they were paraded by **VP** everywhere they went, with strict instructions to everyone else: **hands off!**

After another long night, Daz and Gaz fell into their respective beds in **VP's** mansion. When they heard the alarm on the Monday morning at six o'clock, they lifted their heavy heads off the pillows to the sound of **VP** whistling from the area of the kitchen.

Daz says to Gaz: "I don't believe he's up at this time of the morning. Sounds as if he's making us a cooked breakfast!"

Gaz replied: "It smells like steak and eggs … again!"

The two mates quickly dressed and headed downstairs. They thought they would creep up on good old **VP** and give him a fright! As they tiptoed towards the open-plan kitchen they discreetly peeped round the open door. There on the table were two plates, each holding the biggest steak in history with **VP** standing, to the side of the table, facing the top of the range cooker, wearing his silk dressing gown and nothing else! In his left hand was the frying pan, with two fried eggs sizzling away, and in his right hand was … **HIS COCK!**

He was pulling away at his enlarged member and, just as he got to the vinegar stroke, he aimed **HIS COCK** at the eggs … covering them with sperm in such a way that it gave them a nice finish!

"Well … f**k me!" screamed Daz. "Well … f**k off!" screamed Gaz.

VP turned to face them … still chugging away with a twisted, contorted expression on his face, which can only be described as a cross between **ECSTASY** and **HORROR!** The two mates proceeded to **KICK F**K** out of **VP,** and finished him off by beating him over the head with the **F****N' FRYING PAN!**

In and out of **VP's** cries of pain and passion, he admitted that he had prepared the eggs the same way each day for the two mates! And then added that he thought that the eggs might go down easier! Ah well, you just can't satisfy some folk!

Daz and Gaz took another **£100** from their host's wallet, as agreed the day before, and I have it on good authority from Daz, that neither he nor Gaz, have ever eaten fried eggs since!

Well, not outside their own homes anyway!

* * *

2. East End Tango

Daz and Gaz were out on the town once again, however on this occasion they found themselves in a nice little service personnel club just off Trafalgar Square where the beer was reasonably priced and the chance to meet up with some new, female serving members was always on the cards!

True to form, two short-haired brunettes came in for a drink and a chat up. Before long, they were sweet-talked by the intrepid duo to join them at the bar. The two mates were suited and booted and the two girls were looking more than just sexy!

After an hour or so all four decided to go to an upmarket bar close by, to continue in their new-found friendship, with flirtations and innuendoes at the high point! Daz and Gaz were rubbing their hands with coded smiles and winks at every opportunity. They were certain they were in for a good night, but there was just one snag.

The girls suggested going over to Leicester Square to an even more upmarket club, where they could dance the night away to some great live bands. It sounded like a great idea, but the boys were beginning to realise these two **dolly birds** could turn out to be very, very, high maintenance!

Another round of drinks was ordered to enable Daz and Gaz to come up with a devious plan, from God only knows where. Let's face it, these two **yo-yos** were not exactly the sharpest tools in the box but, hey, on this occasion they were determined not to fail.

Just next to them at the bar, a small bespectacled man in his early thirties was enjoying what appeared to be a cocktail of some kind. He appeared to be weighing up the situation regarding the two girls. He may have had a few quid in his pocket, but that didn't give him the right to make a move on the potential free for all that the two mates had been bankrolling up to now.

All of a sudden, the newcomer gave Daz a dubious, prolonged wink and produced a huge bundle of paper money to pay for his next drink. Both friends were very quick to catch on what was obviously on offer. It wasn't the company of the two **dolly birds** that he wanted it was **Daz …** or maybe it was **Gaz …** or maybe he wanted them both … or maybe he wanted them all!

Gaz whispered to Daz that on the next time the fruit with the four eyes went to the bogs that he, Daz that is, should follow him and give him what he deserves: a good **f****n' kickin'!** Oh yes. And relieve him of his bundle of cash.

Daz was a bit apprehensive but, Gaz soon persuaded him that, if they were to score with the two certs, then the deed had to be done, and sooner rather than later. Gaz would escort the girls outside, hail a taxi and all four would make a quick getaway and absolutely no one would be the wiser!

And Gaz also added that maybe that's what the fruity little bollocks was after anyway. **Rough and ready!** He would probably cream his **f****n' knickers!** Daz was so elated with Gaz's enthusiasm and planning that he agreed to man up and show his mate what he was made of!

Sure enough, the four-eyed fruit gave Daz a cheeky little grin, followed by an even cheekier little wink, then nodded in the direction of the gents' toilet and, in short sharp paces, made his way to the land of **Willy Watchers** with Daz a short distance behind him, with fleeting glances over each shoulder, to make sure that no one would be immediately suspicious of the foul deed that was about to take place.

On entering the gents' toilet, Daz scanned the area completely to ensure of the privacy required for the necessary to take place. The four-eyed fruit was in the first cubicle on the left, opposite the urinals, sinks and mirrors, with absolutely no one else in sight.

Daz entered the cubicle and his new-found friend was standing there, his willy out of his zip, coaxing it to life with short sharp pulls of his right hand, and with a cheeky little grin on his cheeky little four-eyed face!

The only thing he said was: "My name is Henry."

Daz let rip straight away with a great big **f****n' haymaker** with his huge right that caught the four-eyed fruit on the left side of his head, which in turn bounced off the metal wall of the small cubicle! The only thing that followed was complete silence!

Daz looked at Henry, Henry looked at Daz.

Henry shook his head a little and at the same time replaced his willy into his trousers and did up the zip. He then removed his spectacles, folded them and put them into the inside pocket of his small, juvenile jacket. He then proceeded to hit Daz with dazzlingly accurate and devastating blows with his hands, then his feet, then all at once!

Daz thought he had single-handedly walked into a **f****n' riot!**

All of a sudden, Henry stuck his head in, which was like a bolt of lightning, and poor old Daz felt as if his whole body was about to fall to pieces. Daz staggered back into the sinks, took one look in the mirror and saw the damage the mini assault team had inflicted upon him. He screamed for his mate and then **ran like f**k** out of the toilets, through the bar and into the busy London street.

When he suddenly found himself at the front of the bar, guess what? His mate, Gaz, was standing beside a taxi with the door open and the two **dolly birds** waiting patiently inside the vehicle.

Gaz shouted: "What took you so long? Did you get the f****n' money?"

Daz answered in only way he knew how, with a great big **f****n' haymaker!**

Gaz went flying on to the flat of his back beside the taxi, with the two **dolly birds** screaming at the taxi driver to pull off, with the taxi driver screaming at the two **dolly birds** to **close the f****n' door!**

The taxi door was closed with an unmerciful bang and then sped off into the busy London traffic, leaving the two gobsmacked mates looking at each other in utter dismay with a small crowd now beginning to gather to watch the climax of this unbelievable sequence of events!

Daz gave Gaz a hand to get up. They both dusted each other down, shook hands and decided to cut their losses, lick their wounds and head back to barracks. On the way, they ensured that they both had the same story, to tell on their return to the duty sergeant at the guard room: that they were both jumped by six, no, make that eight – yes, eight – civvies but managed to hold their own and make it back to barracks!

As they made their way along Buckingham Place Road, Gaz looked at his watch, looked at the nearest pub and said to Daz: "Mate … fancy a quick pint?"

Daz looked at the sign on the outside of the pub, which read **The Bag O' Nails.**

He then said to Gaz: "Mate … you can f**k right off!"

The Life and Times of Big Jim

1. Question Time

Big Jim went for a job interview with the Army Careers Office. The sergeant at the reception desk and Big Jim had the following conversation.

Sgt: What's your date of birth?

Big Jim: The 15th of the 12th.

Sgt: What year?

Big Jim: Every F*****G year!

Sgt: How many A-levels have you got?

Big Jim: Fourteen!

Sgt: F*****G fourteen! You must be F*****G joking!

Big Jim: Well, you F*****G started it!

Sgt: OK smart arse! Who was half man and half animal?'

Big Jim: Buffalo Bill!

Sgt: Right Dick Head! Do you or do you not want to join the Army?

Big Jim: Why, is it falling apart?

Sgt: Right now! What religion are you?

Big Jim: I'm an atheist.

Sgt: What's a F*****G atheist?

Big Jim: Someone who goes to a Celtic versus Rangers match to watch the F*****G football!

Sgt: Did job seekers send you here?

Big Jim: Yes!

Sgt: Are you seeking a job?

Big Jim: No!

Sgt: Then why have you come in here?

Big Jim: It's raining outside so I thought I would come in here to keep dry!

Sgt: Do your parents know you're here?

Big Jim: Not unless you tell them!

Sgt: Are you sure you've got parents?

Big Jim: Not really. They came round our house collecting for Barnardo's and me ma gave me away!

Sgt: Why are you wasting my time?

Big Jim: I don't see anybody else here!

Sgt: Why don't you just F**k off then?

Big Jim: I would if I could, but I can't!

Sgt: Why can't you?

Big Jim: Because I'm blind in my right ear!

Sgt: And what's wrong with your left ear?

Big Jim: Not a thing. It can see perfectly well!

Sgt: Why don't you just go home?

Big Jim: OK then.

Sgt: If you run all the way home behind the bus you can save £1.50.

Big Jim: If I run behind a taxi I'll save nearly a tenner!

On the way out of the office Big Jim noticed a sign on the wall. **Join the Army! And be alert!**

Big Jim thought to himself: "Should I join the Army? 'Cause the Army needs lerts!"

* * *

2. Drive Time with Mo

Big Jim's sister, Mo, decided to learn to drive a lot later in life than most people. She sometimes had difficulty in understanding the concept of the Highway Code and other drivers' road sense.

When Mo bought her first car Big Jim asked: What kind of car did you buy?

Mo: A blue one!

Big Jim: Is it diesel or petrol?

Mo: I don't know what religion it is!

Big Jim: What was the worst experience when you started your driving lessons?

Mo: I opened up the door to let out the clutch!

Big Jim: Are your indicators working?

Mo: Ach well! Off and on!

Big Jim: Have you tested your air brakes?

Mo: I tried to drive off the end of Belfast Docks, but the driving instructor said he was feeling seasick!

Big Jim: Why were you driving up a one-way street the wrong way?

Mo: I was only going the one way!

Big Jim: Didn't you see the arrows?

Mo: I didn't even see the F*****G Indians!

Big Jim: Do you ever reverse park?

Mo: Don't be so bloody disgusting!

Big Jim: Do you ever suffer from road rage?

Mo: Of course I don't suffer from road rage! Ya dopey F****R! It's all them other F*****G EEjits that don't know how to F*****G drive! Now F**K off!

* * *

3. Drive Time Again with Mo

Mo decides after many years of driving second-hand cars to buy a brand new one. She was lucky enough to come into an unexpected windfall and asked her brother, Big Jim, to come with her to one of the **fourteen** car show rooms she had visited over the previous few weeks.

Big Jim reluctantly agreed, as he knew it would be unwise to decline the very kind offer from his beloved sister!

On their arrival at the said car show room, they were greeted by a middle-aged, grey-haired, follicly-challenged salesman with the biggest false smile you could ever imagine! His smile changed to total horror when he recognised Mo!

Mo's immediate reaction was to say under her breath: "Jim! His eyes are far too close together, but he has the car I want!"

Big Jim just nodded in agreement.

After a quick **Hail Mary**, the **smarmy salesman** tried to make them feel at home with an offer of a comfortable leather armchair, a cup of tea and a biscuit each. There was a selection of three cars for Mo to look at in the colour and price range that had been discussed on her **previously-never-to-be-forgotten-visit!**

As the salesman began his patter, Mo ushered him to one side with a gentle, **Queen-like wave!**

Accompanied with a glance of annoyance with her **matron-like face!**

She had already made her mind up that it was the nice dark blue car that she wanted and **Gurney Gob** was not going to have any further input, apart from the method of payment and the any other paperwork that might arise.

Now, Mo had a test drive on her last visit to the showroom, but was not entirely sure how all the nitty-gritty bits worked, so she relented and allowed **Smarmy Bollocks** to point out all the necessaries to her and Big Jim. Mo sat behind the steering wheel, while big Jim sat next to her in the passenger seat.

A shout from the reception desk by the not-so-well-spoken, illiterate, spotty excuse for a female member of the species prompted **Bald Eagle** to retire temporarily, to wipe the sweat from his brow and have a well-earned break from the delicate proceedings he had the misfortune to be supervising!

While he was away, Mo and Big Jim discussed a particular button that had not yet been explained to them, so Mo pressed it in fully to see what would happen. Apart from a little green light on the dashboard **absolutely nothing!!**

Mo: What's the use of a button that doesn't do anything?

Big Jim: I don't know, Mo!

Mo: You're not much bloody good, are ya? What was the point of you comin' anyway? Ya big dopey bollocks!

Big Jim: I don't know, Mo!

Then, slowly but surely, they both got this uneasy feeling. It started at the back of their legs, then up and around their hips. At this point the couple simultaneously **broke silent-but-deadly wind!**

Both sets of eyes began to bulge as the uneasy warmth came over them. It had made its way around their **arses**, up to their waistlines and was gradually engulfing their lower backs!

The couple then had the same thought: "Have I followed through?"

"Everything OK?" said a familiar voice.

The reptile-featured baldy had returned to engage once

again in the tournament of wills! He couldn't help but notice the unusual whiff from within the vehicle.

"Ah," he said. "I see you've found the seat-warming button. Absolute luxury, don't you think?"

The steam of frustration began to flush all over Mo's face! She took one look at Big Jim and said: "I knew! I knew! I knew what it was all along. What were you worrying about ya big dopey bollocks!"

Big Jim replied: "I don't know, Mo!"

Warning! To all road users: Mo has now got herself a new car! May the force go with you! Amen!

* * *

4. Roast Chicken with Clare

Big Jim's mammy and daddy had paid for a short break at the seaside. A few days before they were due to leave, it dawned on Mammy that it was Great Uncle Mick's 79th birthday while she was on holiday. Uncle Mick's birthday fell on the Sunday of the weekend that Mammy and Daddy would be away. Panic-stricken, she made the following last-minute arrangements: Big Jim and his intended, Clare, would sort out a Sunday roast for Uncle Mick on his birthday.

Now Clare was still a teenager and was not an experienced cook at the best of times, but Mammy was sure she would rally to the cause and try her best.

Mammy had moved into a new multistorey flat with all the mod cons, so roast chicken would be the easiest thing for Clare to cook.

Spuds in one pot.

Sprouts in another pot.

Cheat with the gravy, i.e Bisto, in another pot.

Chicken in the oven and, easy peasy … it's job done!

When Big Jim and Clare were informed of the task in hand, Big Jim just smiled and Clare began to shake! Brendan, who was Big Jim's wee brother and was aged about 14, would also be on hand and assured Clare that he would gladly give a helping hand.

Anyway, off Mammy and Daddy went for a well-earned long weekend at the seaside.

On the big day everything seemed to go according to plan …

Spuds in one pot.

Sprouts in another pot.

Gravy in another pot.

Chicken in the oven.

Brendan then had a brainwave: **Aha! Turn on the cooker!**

At about two o'clock that afternoon, Uncle Mick arrived a wee bit worse for wear. He had spent a few hours in one of his many haunts, celebrating his birthday with a few of his old cronies.

When he sat down in his favourite armchair, Big Jim offered him a glass of whiskey.

Clare whispered: "Make it a big one and give him another. I need all the help I can get!"

After the third very large whiskey, Clare announced that dinner would be five minutes. While Big Jim gave Uncle Mick a hand to get out of the armchair, Brendan gave Clare a hand in the kitchen.

Brendan put spuds on the plates.

Brendan put sprouts on the plates.

Clare removed the chicken from the oven.

Clare began to separate the legs and wings from the chicken.

Clare began to notice sticky red stuff on her fingers … then sticky red stuff on her hands … then sticky red stuff making its way on to her wrists … **BLOOD!**

Brendan whispered: "I think it's still alive!"

Big Jim whispered: "I think it's fighting back!"

Brendan whispered: "It's still a bit cold!"

Big Jim whispered: "Put a duffle coat on it!"

Clare whispered: "Give Uncle Mick another whiskey!"

Then Brendan had a brainwave: let's use the brand new, deep fat fryer that Mammy got just the other day. Brendan had watched Mammy and knew exactly how to use it!

Clare smiled with relief at her potential saviour. Then Brendan put the deep fat fryer on at full blast.

Clare continues to pull the rubbery chicken apart as best she can.

Big Jim gives Uncle Mick another glass of whiskey. Gives himself one, too!

Soon, the fat in the deep fat fryer is hot. Soon the fat is even hotter.

Clare dumps the parts of the chicken, big and small, into the hotter than hot fat.

The chicken goes: **SIZZLE! SIZZLE! SIZZLE!**

Uncle Mick goes: **Hiccup! Hiccup! Hiccup!**

Big Jim goes: **FOR! F***S! SAKE!**

Out comes the chicken absolutely roasting hot … beside the now lukewarm spuds and sprouts, topped off with lukewarm gravy!

LOVELY GRUB!

Three sets of eyes were now transfixed on Uncle Mick. Well now, he tucked in like a scavenger, possessed with the determination of the devil! All three sighed with relief until …

Uncle Mick tried the chicken.

He chewed and chewed! He even took his false teeth out and sucked and sucked!

Brendan tried a mouthful of chicken. It was like trying to eat twigs from a bush!

Clare poured more gravy on to Uncle Mick's plate!

Brendan tried to mash it all up!

Big Jim gave him another whiskey!

Uncle Mick fell asleep!

When he woke up a couple of hours later he complained that his throat felt as if he had been eating leather.

Clare said, with a very straight face: "Uncle Mick, it must be the drink!"

The Life and Times of Joe and Bert

1. Swinging with Bearskins

Joe and Bert were serving in the Army together and were posted to **Windsor.** Ever since their basic training at the guards they had been the best of pals. One Saturday night they went out to the local pub called the Round Tower, which was known as a watering hole for the local totty!

After quite a few jars, the **Dutch** courage kicked in and the two mates decided to chat up a pair of good-looking women sitting at the bar, who had been knocking back **Bacardi** and cokes for most of the night. Both had short dark hair and wore tit-hugging tops, short skirts and high-heeled shoes that enhanced both sets of long sexy legs! The two women were immediately impressed by the chat-up lines, especially from Joe, who could sweet talk the knickers off a **nun!**

Joe and Bert offered the women a drink, which was guzzled down in no time at all! The normal name exchange took place and it wasn't long before they paired off and began dancing to the slow sexy music on the jukebox, which Joe had conveniently played just as the two women had finished the first of the free **Bacardi** and cokes. The women were called Sue and Kate and, would you believe it, they were sisters!

Bert thought … **that's nice**. But in Joe's case, **all sorts of fantasies were flying through his mind!**

Both the boys were really impressed at how the women were reacting to their manly gyrations, although it has to be said that the women, when seen up close and personal, were of, shall we say, a more mature nature and not as young as they first appeared to be.

Joe and Bert had a quick conflab in the gents between gyrations and agreed that it wouldn't be long before their beer goggles arrived and the age of the women wouldn't be an issue. **Ho! Ho! Ho!**

Sue let it slip that she lived locally and just before last orders Joe suggested that they buy a carry out from the pub and continue the movement back at her place. The women agreed, the booze was bought and off they went arm in arm:

Joe with Sue and Bert with Kate, just like true courting couples. Ah, bless.

As they made their way to Sue's place, Joe explained their roll within their **regiment** during **ceremonial duties,** especially at **Windsor Castle!** Sue and Kate were suitably impressed and Sue suggested that the boys nip into barracks to pick up their **ceremonial headdress**, i.e. their **bearskins**, and give the girls a demonstration of their **drill skills!** Joe instructed the women to wait in a shop doorway with Bert while he got their **bearskins**.

Joe then begins to brief Bert of his daring plan:

"Right Bert, you stay here with the women and I'll nip in and nip out again with the bearskins. OK?"

Bert thinks for a moment and then says: "Listen mate, why do they want us to get our bearskins?"

Joe scratches the back of his head and speaks in a very soft but reassuring tone: "Listen Dopey! These two women want to see us in our bare skins, wearing our bearskins!

F**k, rattle and roll!"

Bert once again thinks for a moment and says: "But Joe, my bearskin is all groomed and ready for the guard mount in the morning!"

Joe replies: "If you want a rave up and a bunk up TOOOONIGHT shut to f**k up and stay here and keep an eye on the booze!"

Bert nods in agreement and says: "Why am I keeping an eye on the booze, mate?"

Joe replies: "Bert! Will you shut the f**k up and just f****n' stay here with the women and the booze, or I will personally set fire to your f****n' bearskin!"

Bert, being slightly shaken by his mate's angry threat, replies: "OK, Joe. Just don't harm my beautiful bearskin. Because, because, because I love it!"

Anyway, Joe nips in and nips out with the two **bearskins**, each hidden in their respective canvas bags. The **guard commander** was a mate and, with a promise from Joe for an update of his **sexploits** on his return to barracks, turned a blind eye!

The waiting trio didn't have long to wait when the slightly puffed out Joe returned with a great big smile on his face!! All four began to make their way to Sue's place, fumbling and feeling anything that could be fumbled or felt!

On arrival at Sue's ground floor maisonette, they all fell through the door giggling and laughing and soon tore into the booze! And, it wasn't just the booze that was making Joe slobber around the chops!

Slowly but surely, various items of clothing were being discarded around the small sitting room and kitchen. As it was Sue's place, Joe bagged the only bedroom and threw a spare pillow and bedspread at Bert and Kate, who by this stage, were in a state of semi-undress on the settee.

For the next hour or so, Joe and Bert were giving it **WHOMPO!**, with and without their **bearskins!**

At about three in the morning, Joe made his way to the toilet for a well-earned piss.

Still wearing, not his, but Bert's **bearskin!** With drink taken and with the lights out, Bert wouldn't know that Joe had made a switch. Consequently, Bert would be extra careful with what he thought was his true love.

They were both on **guard mount** that morning! Joe might be sex mad, but not mad all together!

* * *

2. It Comes to Those who Wait

There was a new night club that opened in Windsor called **Blazers**. The word was out that the management were recruiting for part-time staff to work nights, some for bar work, some to wait on tables and some to work in Dixie Land (washing dishes).

Joe and Bert jumped at the chance to earn some extra money, pinch a few free drinks and maybe further their **sexploits** with the local female **Windsorians!**

The two mates quickly applied for the jobs and, lo and behold, with Bert paying attention and Joe doing all the talking, they were to start the following Monday night on a trial basis. They would be part of the waiter service, bringing food and drinks to the tables in their designated areas. They were also required to keep the tables as clean and tidy as possible throughout the night's **cabaret** and, later, throughout the **disco**.

All they had to do was to show up on the night for a one-hour walk-through, talk-through and, bingo, yer job's a good one! They had to arrive clean and tidy wearing white, long-sleeve shirts, black bow ties, black trousers and highly polished shoes! **No probs** for these two experienced **guardsmen!**

The two mates were a tremendous success and were offered a minimum of three nights a week each for the foreseeable future. They would sometimes be very busy for long periods of their shift but the money wasn't bad, the **cabaret** and **disco** were great, plus there were a few free drinks and, in most cases, a bit of **ruff luv**, to round off the night!

After a few weeks they were given a chance to show their skills in the **VIP room**.

This was a special room behind the stage where all the artists for the **cabaret** and **disco** were entertained before, during and after the night's performance. Now, this was a crème de la crème job and held lots of potential perks! Once again, Joe began to slobber around the chops!

A well-known female **pop singer** at the time was the **star act** that night. She was petite, sexy, and drop dead gorgeous, wearing the most minute miniskirt known to man! And, of course, she was also wearing **FMBs – Fuck Me Boots!**

The two mates looked at each other, and Joe said to Bert: "I'd use her shite for toothpaste and her piss for mouthwash!"

Bert replied: "I wouldn't go that far, mate. I just want to do her some serious damage!"

Anyway, the whole night couldn't have gone better. The performers were all in great form and the **star act** was so down to earth. There were plenty of hangers-on for Joe and Bert to chat up and also enjoy a drink. The work rate was fairly easy compared to that on the tables, so it was almost like a free night out and being paid at the same time!

The **star act** had to perform twice throughout the show, each set lasting about an hour. She had about forty-five minutes between each set but still, thirsty work!

It was up to Joe and Bert to keep the trays of snacks topped up and, of course, keep the drinks flowing. As this was the last night of this particular show's run for the week, there would be an after show party, to which the two mates were invited to stay on.

At about half past one in the morning, the after show party really began to kick off!

Dancing, drinking, debauchery galore!

It was like a game of pass the parcel, except it was pass the ARSE!

Just as the two mates were about to get their fair share, the **star act** began cursing and swearing that nobody was paying her the proper attention! A few insults were exchanged, a few drinks were thrown, a few handbags at ten paces were also thrown.

The **PA** to the **star act (who could have been mistaken for the pop singer's sister)**, took control of the situation and guided the fallen star to a more private room.

Bert was feeling a bit sorry for the **PA** and, with a helping hand, steadied the **star act** down the short flight of stairs to a waiting taxi. But then disaster struck! The very nice down to earth lady from earlier in the night began to scream that Bert was touching her up! Bert glanced round to see if Joe was following but he was nowhere to be seen!

At this stage, Joe had his tongue down one woman's throat, with another woman stood by to take over the lashing of his tongue, when he came up for air. So, he didn't give a **monkey's f**k** about anything else!

Thankfully, the **drunken bitch** with the **PA** passed out and Bert assisted both into the back of the waiting car.

Bert thought to himself: Thank f**k for that. I'm off the hook now.

But, alas! This was not to be.

The **PA** asked Bert to help her to get her boss back to their hotel and into her room. Poor ol' Bert couldn't say no. It wasn't in his nature.

So, off all three went in the back of the taxi and in a few minutes all three were standing outside the hotel, with the

drunken bitch hanging on to Bert, with her arms clasped behind his neck in a head lock.

Bert thought to himself: "Where's that bastard Joe when I need him? And to think I fancied the knickers off this bitch at the start of the night!"

About ten minutes later, the **PA** was opening the door to her boss's room. Without further ado, the **pop singer** was sprawled out on the bed, sleeping soundly in her drunken stupor!

At this stage, Bert mumbled a good night but the **PA** asked if he would like a night cap. Although slightly surprised at the offer, poor ol' Bert couldn't say no. It wasn't in his nature.

The **PA** opened the door to the adjoining hotel room and motioned for Bert to follow her through. In no time at all they were helping themselves to the well-stocked **mini-bar**. And, as the PA was equally well stocked, Bert made his first move … to give her a gentle kiss. At first she pulled back, but only to put the radio on, and return to his warm embrace.

Bert: "Do you not sing or dance like your boss?"

PA: "I don't sing, but I do like to dance. Especially with my knight in shining armour."

Bert: "F**k the dance. Do you want to see my lance?"

I think she got the point!

The next morning, when Bert got up … well, he was well up on more than one occasion. Nevertheless, he was still late for work!

When he and Joe met up for a tea break later that morning, Joe asked: “Are you still hung over from last night mate?”

Bert replied: “You have no idea what’s still hung over from last night mate! Hee, hee, hee!

Heartbreak Hotel

Tony was a Belfast man who had been living and working in and around the London area for more years than he cared to remember. He worked mostly in the building industry but over the long hard years he became a very sought after and highly qualified scaffolder.

He had his fair share of women over the years and been in more than just a few bar brawls. Yes, Tony had certainly been around the hot spots. Drinking hot spots and female hot spots, if you know what I mean! **Hee! Hee!**

Now, when Tony finished a hard week's work it was straight to his local pub for a well-earned drink with his mates. They would always wind him up about his age, as he was the boss and most of his workmates were getting younger **and Younger**.

On one particular rowdy night, a crowd of young female students from a local university were out on the lash and also on the prowl. When the girls set eyes on all these young **VIRILE HE MEN** they couldn't believe their luck!

Drinks and Sex a Plenty!

"Oh Yes," said the girls.

"Bring it on,' said the boys.

As the night wore on, Tony realised that he was probably the oldest person in the pub! Just about everyone else was young enough to be his offspring! Tony's young mates were singing and dancing and telling Tony that he would be going home on his own that night!

Suddenly, a tall, long-haired brunette approached Tony, said her name was Lucy, and began to strike up a conversation. She was drop-dead gorgeous and, as it transpired in their conversation, was only 19 years of age!

Tony immediately thought that it was a wind-up! After an hour or so, Lucy had made it very clear, that she was attracted to older men! She suggested that they go elsewhere. Anywhere really, just to get away from the noise in the pub, which it has to be said had reached fever pitch!

Tony left the pub with Lucy, to the sound of wolf whistles and chants of **you jammy old bastard!** His small ground floor flat was only a few minutes' walk away so in no time they were at it like two dogs on heat!

They started to undress each other as they went through the front door.

They were **clutching and clawing** and **grunting and panting** and **slobbering and slithering** …

Into every **crease and crevice**, as if the following day was going to be the end of the world!

Their first session lasted for more than an hour.

Over and over … up and down … in and out … round and round … sound as a pound!

After a brief rest, a cigarette and a family-sized measure of Irish whiskey each, it was time for round two. And what a round this turned out to be.

As Tony positioned himself between her legs she moaned: "Tony … Tony … show me how hard you really are."

Tony looked down and said: "This is as hard as it gets!"

And then the conversation went as follows:

Lucy: I want you to show me some force.

Tony: What do you mean?

Lucy: Hit me when we make love. Push it up inside me and then thump my head with your fist at the same time!

Tony: Are you sure?

Lucy: Yes … yes… do it now. Thump and f**k me. Thump and f**k. Thump and f**k. Yes!

Tony: You know me. Anything to oblige! Yahoo!

Lucy: Tony, thump me harder … harder … harder!

They were now at the point of no return. Tony gave her a great big haymaker and, lo and behold … she passed out.

F*****g knocked out to be precise!

Tony's joystick took an immediate nosedive!

Tony tried to bring her round, but no such luck!

Tony began to panic. He felt her pulse. She was still alive! What was he to do?

The left side of her face was beginning to swell up and was becoming discoloured with every passing second!

She needed medical attention. Tony phoned for an ambulance. While he was waiting for help he began to throw some water on her face and she began to stir.

Bang! Bang! Bang!

The ambulance was at the door. Tony quickly lifted Lucy off the bed and placed her on her left side on the floor. She was now slightly coherent and she agreed to say that she had fallen out of bed!

The ambulance crew were very sympathetic, and equally very sceptical, that a fall out of bed would result in the side of her face looking like a monkey's arse!

But, fortunately for Tony, both of the crew were regulars at the pub that he was at earlier.

Nudge Nudge! Wink Wink!

Tony never met up with Lucy again. The ambulance crew informed Tony that, although she was in need of serious attention, she returned to her studies soon after their night of passion, but had to return to the outpatients' department for follow-up treatment for her jaw …

Which was fractured in two places!!!

* * *

The Famous Irish

All the over the world there are famous **Irish** people or famous **Irish** descendants!

Take singers for example, there's the Irish Americans:

Neil O'Diamond.

John O'Denver.

And that great Irish Australian singer: **Olivia Newton O'John!**

Now, Olivia was a direct descendant of that very well-known **Irish** explorer:

Sir Walter O'Reilly:

Who introduced us to Park Drive, Woodies and the Irish mixed grill: roast potatoes, mashed potatoes, boiled potatoes and chips!

Now, Sir Walter was a second cousin of that very well-known Indian chief: Chicken Soup, last of the O'Hagans.

He, in turn, was a distant relation to that other very well-known Indian warrior: Chief Sitting Still!

He was the one that wiped out the Irish imposters at the battle of: Your man with the Big Horn: General Custard!

Now, General Custard's favourite war cry was: Lucky f****n' seven!

There was a song written about the massacre and was recorded by that very well-known Irish Showband: Big Bo and the Arrowheads.

Guess what, it reached number seven and stayed there for seven weeks!

So, after all that just remember, it was General Custard with his Long Blonde Ringlets, on his big horse, with his big hat, with his big lunch pack, that drove all those wild Indians into an absolute frenzy!

And as we all now know, that was the basis upon which that very well-known Irish band was formed:

Yes, you got it in one: **THE INDIANA JOES!**

* * *

Stand-up Comedy (The old ones are always the best)

Mick and Pat, who were from **Cavan**, thought they would try their hand at counterfeiting. They were trying to make **£20** notes, unfortunately when they printed the notes they came out as **£18** notes!

Anyway, they decided to take all the notes they had printed, pack them into two suitcases and try their luck in Belfast. When they got there, they went to Royal Avenue to find a bank.

Mick: Pat, you take one of the £18 notes into the bank and see how you get on.

Pat: Are you sure they will take one of these notes?

Mick: Of course I am, Pat. Sure these Belfast EEJITS will take anything!

So, Pat opens up one of the suitcases and takes out one of the £18 notes. He leaves Mick with the suitcases and goes into the bank, goes up to the counter and says to the man: "Excuse me, sir, could you change this £18 note?"

The man looks at Pat and says: "Of course I can. How would you like it? two nines, three sixes, or six feckin' threes!"

* * *

Mick and Pat had agreed to meet down by the river for a day's fishing.

When Mick arrived Pat was already there, but to Mick's astonishment, Pat had brought along his mother-in-law!

Mick took Pat to one side and said: "In the name of all that's holy Pat, Why in GOD'S name did you bring your feckin' mother-in-law with you?"

Pat replied: "Sure she's very useful, Mick."

"What do you mean she's very useful?" says Mick. "Did she bring the sandwiches?"

"No," says Pat.

"Did she bring the tea?" says Mick.

"No," says Pat.

"Did she bring the beer?" says Mick.

"No," says Pat.

"Then why is she so feckin' useful?" says Mick.

"She's got feckin' worms," says Pat.

* * *

Benny and Ester from Belfast were having a wee drink one day in the local pub, celebrating a wee win on the oul gees gees. They were becoming a wee bit tipsy and began to get lovey-dovey.

Ester asked: "Benny love, if anything ever happened to me, I mean, if I was ill and passed away and you were left on your own, would you find somebody else?"

Benny: "Well, after a wee while, somebody might come along, I'm not too sure."

Ester: "Well if you did, would you make love to her?"

Benny: "Well, I might."

Ester: "Would you, use our bed?"

Benny: "Well, I might."

Ester: "Would you let her use my golf clubs?"

Benny: "No feckin' way love. SHE'S LEFT HANDED!"

* * *

Jean Pierre was a famous French pilot who was at the Farnborough Air Show.

On the first night he takes a beautiful blonde back to his hotel room. When they are naked on the bed he pours white wine all over her tits.

The blonde screams: "Jean Pierre, Jean Pierre, what are you doing?"

To which he replies: "I am Jean Pierre the famous French peelot. When I make lourve to a beautiful blonde laidee, I suck white wine off her nipellza."

On the second night he takes a beautiful black girl back to his hotel room. When they are naked on the bed he pours red wine all over her belly.

The black girl screams: "Jean Pierre, Jean Pierre, what are you doing?"

To which he replies: "I am Jean Pierre, the famous French peelot. When I make lourve to a beautiful black laidee, I suck wine from her navull."

On the third night he takes a beautiful redhead back to his hotel room. When they are naked on the bed he pours lighter fuel all over her minge and strikes a match to set her on fire.

The redhead screams: "Jean Pierre, Jean Pierre, what are you doing?"

To which he replies: "I am Jean Pierre, the famous French peelot. When I go down, I go down in flames!"

* * *

Sammy had a great wee win on the horses! He decided instead of spending it on drink he would take himself off somewhere different for a weekend trip. He got a great deal for a four-day weekend break to Paris. He kept his plans to himself as he still had plenty of money left for booze and maybe a visit to one of those fancy massage parlours!

Poor Sammy thought the big day would never come, what with the left over cash burning a hole in his pocket for nearly two weeks!

At last, he was on the plane to Paris! No sooner had he arrived when he headed straight to the nearest bar, whereupon he went straight on the rip! He couldn't help but notice all the jammy bastards around him with sexy women swapping spit like there was no tomorrow!

He spoke to the barman and explained how he wanted to sample the delights of a French masseur. The barman assured him that it was a French masseuse that would fulfil his fantasies (masseuse is a female!).

So, without further ado, Sammy followed the directions given by the barman and within only a few minutes he was at the front door of a dimly lit club in a dimly lit side street.

Once inside he approached the front desk and spoke to a very well-endowed brunette with red cherry lips: she just oozed temptation: at the highest level!

She spoke good English and in no time at all he was in a very small, dimly lit private room.

Sammy sat on the small chair in the corner, opposite a narrow, trolley-type bed, which was covered in a white sheet. Then, in she came! The feckin' French masseuse!

She looked very young, had short blonde hair and wearing an even shorter nurse's uniform, with white stilettos … with legs all the way up to her arse! The top of her uniform was undone almost to her waist … just about covering her petite girlie titties. Sammy almost filled his boxers!

She then said: "If you would lika de massage, you must taka all your cloothes off!"

Sammy mumbled: "Dead on, wee girl!"

In a microsecond Sammy was bollock naked.

She then said: "Lie face a down on de bed."

Sammy obeyed instantly.

She then asked: "Would you lika me to massage your shouldeers?"

Sammy says: "Yes please."

She says: "Would you lika me to massage your back?"

Sammy says: "Yes please."

She says: "Would you lika me to massage your boottocks?"

Sammy says: "Yeeees please."

She then rubs his arse and then gently inserts a finger into his quivering hole! This sends a shiver up Sammy's spine!

She says: "Would you lika to turn oover?"

Sammy says: "OOOH yeeees please."

So, Sammy turns over! His now fully erect member is in all its glory, swaying slightly just like an upside down pendulum!

She then says: "Would you lika de WANK?"

Sammy says: "OOOH yeeees please."

She leaves the room for about five minutes and when she returns she says: "Ave you finnnisstt?"

* * *

Dopey Shuey needs a second-hand door for the back of his Ford van. He calls into the garage to ask what price it might be. When he arrived at the garage he was greeted by the owner, who asked if he could be of assistance.

Dopey Shuey: "Do ya have any second-hand doors for sale that would fit me wee Ford van?"

Owner: "Yes I have."

Dopey Shuey: "How much are they?"

Owner: "£20 each, and well worth the money."

Dopey Shuey: "They're only £10 up the feckin' road!"

Owner: "Why didn't ya buy one up the feckin' road then?"

Dopey Shuey: "They had none feckin' left."

Owner: "Ours will be £10, when we've got none feckin' left!"

Dopey Shuey: "All right, I'll come back when you've got none feckin' left!

* * *

Two dogs met up at the Dublin dog show, one was a female poodle and the other was a male mongrel.

They made small talk and then the mongrel asks: “How did you get on at the show?”

To which the poodle replied: “I got one first, two seconds and highly commended. How did you get on?”

To which the mongrel replied: “I got one f**k, two fights and HIGHLY DELIGHTED!”

* * *

Did you hear about the Irishman who opened up a bar on the MOON?

He closed it down. There was NO ATMOSPHERE!

Why are Irish jokes so silly?

So Englishmen can understand them!

There’s no such thing as an Irish joke.

They’re all true stories!

Why was Jesus Christ never born in Ireland?

They couldn’t find a Virgin and Three Wise Men!

What’s the odd one out: A thick Irishman, an intelligent Irishman or a dinosaur?

The thick Irishman, because the other two are extinct!

* * *

The Queen was on a visit to Australia when the over-familiar Australian prime minister puts his arm around her waist and says: "Do ya know somethin' Mam, we're thinkin' of becomin' a Kingdom."

To which the Queen replied: "You have to have a king to become a kingdom."

The prime minister then says: Strewth, then we'll become a bloody principality!

To which the Queen replies: "You have to have a prince to become a principality."

The prime minister is stunned for a moment, when the Queen then adds: "I'll tell you what prime minister. Why don't you just remain a CUNTRY!"

* * *

I had a dream! And in that dream, I dreamed that Ireland and England were playing in the final of the Rugby World Cup. And in that dream, the final was being played at Raven Hill in Belfast.

I found myself wandering towards the venue looking for a ticket tout to sell me a ticket, when I finally met up with one on a street corner.

He said: “I have only one ticket left!”

So, I said: “And how much are ya chargin’ for that one ticket left?”

He said: “£250!”

So, I said: “250 bloody quid. Sure I could get the sexiest woman in Belfast for that amount of money.”

He said: “Ahh! But wud ya get 40 minutes each way with a band playin’ in the feckin’ middle!”

* * *

Wee Johnny was at school when Miss Moss the teacher decided to test the class with some mental arithmetic.

Miss Moss: "Now Johnny, if I were to give you two ducks, a pair of ducks and a couple of ducks, how many ducks would you have?"

Johnny: "S-S-S-Seven Miss."

Miss Moss smiled and asked the question again: "Now, Now," says she. "If I were to give you two ducks, a pair of ducks and a couple of ducks, how many ducks would you have?"

Johnny: "S-S-S-Seven Miss."

Miss Moss decided to try a different approach: "Johnny," says she. "If I were to give you two chickens, a pair of chickens and a couple of chickens, how many chickens would you have?"

Johnny: "Six Miss."

"Right," she thought: "He's got the hang of it at last." "Now Johnny! If I were to give you two ducks, a pair of ducks and a couple of ducks, how many ducks would you have?"

Johnny: "S,-S-S-Seven Miss!"

Miss Moss: "How do you work that out?"

Johnny: "Ahh Miss … Sure I have a duck at home!"

* * *

There were two men from the wilds of West Cork, Barney and Davey, sitting in a bar in London, having just arrived on the boat train from Ireland.

After having three or four pints of Guinness to settle themselves before asking for directions to their digs, Barney noticed a very large mirror at the other side of the room facing Davey's back. They had never seen a mirror before!

Barney leans across the table and whispers to Davey: "Don't look now but there's two blokes at the other side of the bar and one of them keeps lookin' at us over here."

Davey glances over his shoulder and says: "F**k me! The two of them are at it now!"

Barney: "I think, we go over there and ask them what they're feckin' lookin at."

Davey nods in agreement and as they both stand up he says: "Hang on! They'er comin' over feckin' here!"

* * *

Billy arrived in Belfast for his uncle Mick's funeral. On going through some old paperwork he'd found in the bottom of an old tin box, Billy found an old crumpled up receipt for a pair of leather brogues that uncle Mick had left in for repair at the local cobblers dating back almost ten years!

Billy decided to locate the cobblers, if it was still there, and redeem the said brogues if, in fact, they were still there.

As luck would have it, Billy found the wee run down oul shop in question and, on going inside, noticed an equally wee run down oul man, behind the counter.

Billy produced the receipt and asked if there would be any chance that the brogues would still be there.

The wee run down oul man glanced at the crumpled piece of paper, shuffled into a back room and, lo and behold, he appeared about five minutes later with a dusty pair of black brogues.

He said: "Here they are son. To be re-soled and heeled, for Mr Mick Sullivan, £5 already paid."

To which Billy asked: "Would it be OK if I took them with me? If they fit then I'd like to wear them to the funeral."

"When's the funeral?" asks the wee man.

"Monday mornin'," says Billy.

"Fraid not," says the wee man. "They won't be ready till Tuesday!"

* * *

Father Murphy was conducting confessions when a sudden urge to succumb to the call of nature flashed through his bowels.

He juked out of the back of the confession box and noticed the newly arrived and newly ordained priest loitering with the intention to picking up a few hints on how to conduct a live confession.

Father Murphy whispered: “Hey boy, get over here right now and take over from me, till I get rid of this dose of the skitters!”

The new priest whispered: “I’ve never done it for real before. What penance do I give for what sins?”

Father Murphy whispered: “Look son, there’s a wee list on the wall at our side of the confession box that will help you out.”

With that the two priests made the changeover. The newly arrived priest studied the help sheet, which gave general guidance for those in doubt, such as:

Telling Mammy lies = 2 × Hail Marys.

Telling Daddy lies = 2 × Our Fathers.

Swearing = 3 × Hail Marys and 3 × Our Fathers.

The list continued, covering every eventuality.

The new priest was ready and willing when the next confessor arrived. He was a wee boy of about 10 years old.

The wee boy: “Bless me Father for I have sinned, etc, etc.”

Every time the wee boy confesses a sin, the new priest

glances at the guide on his side of the wall and adds up in his mind's eye just what to award the wee boy at the end of his confession.

The wee boy keeps the worst sin to the end and said: "I had a wank, father."

The new priest: "You had a what?"

The wee boy: "I had a wank, father."

The new priest scanned the guide looking for the word wank but he just couldn't find it!

He began to panic! He stuck his head out of the back of the confession box and saw an altar boy sweeping up.

The new priest whispered to the altar boy: "What does Father Murphy give for a wank?"

The altar boy shouted: "A can of Coke and a Mars bar, father!"

* * *

Billy and Paddy had been mates for years in the Army. They both decided to return to Belfast and retire. Billy returned to Sandy Row and Paddy to the Falls Road.

After a few months, Billy contacted Paddy and invited him to the Twelfth celebrations at his house in Sandy Row and then to watch the parade as it passed Shaftesbury Square.

Paddy thought this was a great idea and accepted Billy's kind invitation.

On arrival in Sandy Row on the day, Paddy noticed a gable wall with football posts painted on it and this gave Paddy a great idea.

He had an old uncle who was raising money for a charity event and suggested to Billy the following:

Paddy: "Why don't I get a football and charge a pound to kick it between the goal posts and raise money for my uncle's charity?"

Billy: "Who's gonna pay a feckin' pound to kick a ball against the wall?"

Paddy: "We can paint a wee picture of Pope John-Paul, on the ball, so …

kick the ball … with John-Paul … against the wall!"

Billy: "Kick the ball … with John-Paul … against the wall! That's sounds great to me. We'll make a fortune for your uncle's charity!

Now, with that the two oul mates proceeded to get the **Pope's** face painted on a football by an obliging neighbour of Billy's, from a colour photo that Paddy had brought with him.

And just to make sure everyone knew it was John-Paul, the word **POPE** was also painted above his face.

Would you believe it? Within a short period of time, there was a queue stretching almost 200 yards up Sandy Row, with little chance of it decreasing as each minute passed!

Billy and Paddy were both taking it in turns to shout: "Roll up! Roll up! Kick the ball … with John-Paul … against the wall! A pound a go, one and all!!"

At the end of the day they had raised more than **£2,000.** They changed most of the coins in the local **Rangers Football Supporters Club** for notes and off Paddy went with the money for his uncle's charity.

The following year Billy, suggested that they carry out the same fundraiser again. He told Paddy that it was requested by many of those who took part, young and old, that it should become an annual event every year for the foreseeable future.

Billy also suggested that they raise the amount per kick to **two pounds!** Paddy just couldn't wait for the next Twelfth.

And soon the great day came. More than the previous year turned up and the money was just rolling in. This time Paddy took away more than **£5,000** to his uncle.

The following year Paddy didn't show up. Billy phoned him and said: "Hey Paddy. Will you hurry up! There's a big crowd down here in Sandy Row. They want to … kick the ball … with John-Paul … against the wall!"

Paddy said: "I won't be comin' this year mate."

Billy shouted: "Why feckin' not!"

Paddy said: "Ah Billy. Sure the chapel has already been built!"

* * *

Did you hear about the Irish wolfhound?

He broke his nose chasing parked cars!

He was chewing a bone and, when he stood up, his left leg fell off!

He walked backwards and wagged his nose!

Did you hear about the **gay Irish wolfhound?**

He kissed cats and barked: **Bowsey Wowsey!**

* * *

On St Patrick's Day, Tim went into a big new fancy bar down town in Belfast.

He said to the girl behind the bar:

Set me up 17 pints of Guinness.

The girl began the slow process of pouring the 17 pints of Guinness. As she began to pour the third pint, she put the first pint on the bar for Tim to begin his celebrations. And so the process continued: A pint of Guinness in Tim's hand, another on the bar and another being poured! No problem!

After about four hours, Tim was just about able to stand with the last of the 17 pints in his hand when he asked the girl: "Do you sell … do you sell … do you sell shorts in this friggin' bar?"

The girl replied: "Of course we do sir!"

Tim said: "Then you had better sell me a friggin' pair, I've just shit these ones!"

The following morning, Tim woke up at about five o'clock with the hangover of all hangovers. And so he decided to commit suicide! He staggered the short distance from his house to the **Albert Bridge,** where he promptly jumped into the **River Lagan.**

It took the **fire service** two hours to dig him out. **The friggin' tide was out!**

* * *

There were two novice nuns cycling down a cobbled stone lane on their way back to the **nunnery.**

One nun said to the other: "I've never come this way before!"

The same two novice nuns were sneaking back to the **nunnery** long after lights out. They were returning from a sly visit to the pub in the village. When they got to the gates they found them to be locked, so they decided to climb over the back wall. As they were both spreadeagled on the top of the wall one novice said to the other novice: "I feel like a commando!"

"Yeh. But where would you get one at this time of the friggin' night?"

Why do nuns always go out in pairs? One nun makes sure, the other nun gets none!

The Mother Superior arrived in the dining hall for breakfast. She was in a foul mood. She screamed at all the nuns, young and old, for more than half an hour for no reason, other than to hear the sound of her own voice!

One senior nun, who was about 80 years of age, waited for a lull in the verbal abuse and asked a question: "Mother Superior, did you get out of the wrong side of the bed this morning?"

The Mother Superior looked over her horn-rimmed glasses and answered the question with a question: "Why do you ask?"

The senior nun replied: "Because you've got Father Kelly's boots on!"

* * *

Barney and Annie were an elderly couple living in Enniskillen. They were reminiscing about the good old days when Annie suggested that whichever one of them died first, he or she should return from the other side to tell the other what it was like. They both agreed that this was, indeed, a great idea!

A year or so later Barney passed away in his sleep and Annie prayed that he would go to heaven and also remember to return and tell her what it was like.

A few weeks later, in the middle of the night, Annie was awakened by a rustling sound in her bedroom. She immediately sat up in bed and tried to switch on her bedside light but it didn't work. Almost panic stricken, she called out: Who's there?

A voice that she instantly recognised softly replied: "It's only me, Annie."

Annie: "My God! It's you Barney!"

Barney: "That's right my love. It's me, Barney."

Annie: "Have you come back to tell me what it's like on the other side?"

Barney: "That's right my love."

Annie: "Well hurry up and tell me!"

Barney: "Well now. Every morning starts with breakfast, then I hop skip and jump round the golf course and then … I have SEX!

"I go for a wee sleep, then I have lunch, then I hop skip and jump round the golf course and then … I have SEX!"

"I go for another wee sleep, then have my dinner, then I hop skip and jump round the golf course and then … I have SEX!

"That my love is what it's like on the other side."

Annie: "Are you in heaven?"

Barney: "No my love. I'm a feckin' big rabbit on the Enniskillen golf course!"

* * *

Wee Slugger goes into a pub with his pet mouse in his breast pocket.

He asks the barman for a pint of lager and two large whiskeys. He takes a large swallow from the lager, then drinks one of the large whiskeys in one gulp.

He then puts the second large whiskey level to his breast pocket, whereupon the pet mouse peeps up, opens his mouth and Wee Slugger slowly pours the booze into the mouse.

A few moments later, Wee Slugger finishes his lager and orders the same round again.

The barman watches and, lo and behold, the same procedure is carried out. The pet mouse never missed a single drop!

After a couple of hours, Wee Slugger is well and truly pissed and tries to start a sing-song. The pet mouse was sticking his head up now and again, out of the breast pocket and looked as if he was joining in!

The Barman: "That's enough now! There's no singin' allowed!"

Wee Slugger: "I'm not singin' aloud. I'm singin' alow."

The Barman: "If you'er goin' to be ignorant about it, you can drink up and go!"

Wee Slugger: "Sing it out your ear, Fat Chops!"

The Barman: "I'll come round there and give you a good feckin' hidin'!"

Wee Slugger: "Come on then, if you think you're big enough!"

The pet mouse pops his head up once more and says: "And if you've got a big fat cat, you can feckin' bring him out, too!"

* * *

Slim Eddie went into the pub in Belfast and ordered two pints of Guinness. He stood alone in the corner of the bar and drank the two pints.

The following night the same thing happened and this continued for nearly a week, until the barman had to satisfy his curiosity and ask Slim Eddie why he ordered two pints of Guinness each night and not one at a time.

Slim Eddie explained: “Well now, ya see, my big brother is doin’ six months in jail, so I order two pints of Guinness, one for me, one for him, and I feel as if he’s right here beside me!”

The barman: “Ach Jasus. Isn’t that a lovely thought. Here, have the next two on the house.”

Slim Eddie continued to use the same pub for many weeks to come, always ordering the same two pints of Guinness every time, until one night he came in and ordered one pint of Guinness!

The barman thought the worst. That something had happened to the big brother.

The barman: “Is everything all right?”

Slim Eddie: “Of course everything is all right. Why do you ask?”

The barman: “You always order two pints of Guinness, one for you, one for him. Your big brother, is he OK?”

Slim Eddie: “My big brother’s fine!”

The barman: “Then why have you only ordered one pint of Guinness?”

Slim Eddie: “Well now, this pint is for my big brother. Sure it’s comin’ up for Easter and I’m off the drink for Lent!”

* * *

Dinky McGlinchie lived and worked on a farm all his life right up until the day he died at 87 years of age. His only surviving relative was his spinster sister, Mary, aged 89.

Mary called into the local newspaper office to put in a wee death notice for the following day. She spoke to the young man in the office called Tommy and he explained how things are normally done.

Tommy: Now Mary, it costs £5 per word to put a death notice into the paper.

Mary: How much?

Tommy: £5 per word.

Mary: That's awful dear young fella.

Tommy: Look Mary, that's the going rate, there's nothing I can do about it.

Mary: Right then! Put this in! "McGlinchie's dead". That's enough said!

Tommy: I'm sorry Mary. The minimum amount of words is five!

Mary: Five bloody words, just to tell people what they already know! That's £25! That's bloody scandalous!

After a short pause Mary says: Right then! Put this in:

"McGlinchie's dead … Volvo for sale."

* * *

Two oul fellas in the village, Ted and Ned, died on the same day. Their remains were moved to the undertakers to be embalmed and dressed prior to the funeral service in the local church.

Ted's sister, Ann, and Ned's sister, Fran, took a suit of clothes for each dead man down to the undertaker, who, due to the drink that was taken over the years, was known as Big Wobbley Bob!

Now, Ann dropped off a navy suit for Ted and Fran dropped off a light grey suit for Ned. Both with matching shirts and ties.

Sure they'll both look the picture of health, agreed the two bereaved women.

The following night, the two dead men, all dressed in their finery in their equally fine coffins, were due to be moved to the local church to spend their last night in the village under the good Lord's roof.

Ann and Fran arrived about an hour early to ensure all was well and that their brothers were presentable for viewing by the large amount of mourners expected to view Ted and Ned before their transportation.

On arrival, they approached their respective brothers in their respective coffins and stood in absolute disbelief at the sight before them!

Ted's navy suit, was worn by Ned, and Ned's light grey suit, was worn by Ted!

Well, Ann and Fran laid into Big Wobbley Bob like two demented banshees!

They were screaming and shouting, cursing and swearing, punching and growling!

After about five minutes, the fallout from the nuclear attack died down to a simmering boil. Big Wobbley Bob was lying on the floor, curled up and whimpering like a baby.

Ann and Fran had a whispered discussion about the misfortune of Ted and Ned.

Ann then said: "If those two men are not dressed in their proper clothes by the time the mourners get here, we will personally caaastrate you and stuff them so far up your arse that you'll have the mumps, for the rest of your days!"

Big Wobbley Bob assured them that he would definitely rectify the problem!

Twenty minutes later, the hearse arrived with the family circle and friends of both men, numbering well over one hundred, to see them off to the church.

Ted and Ned looked great in their proper suits. To Ann and Fran's pleasant surprise Big Wobbley Bob had even managed to change the shirts and ties as well!

After the funeral and burial the following day, Ann and Fran approached Big Wobbley Bob and inquired how he managed to change the suits, shirts and ties so quickly?

Big Wobbley Bob announced with great pride and delight: "Aaah sure. We just changed the heads!"

* * *

Joey the binman was on his rounds on a wet, cold and windy Monday morning. He was nursing his usual Monday morning hangover!

Normally, if the wheelie bins were not out for emptying on time, he would just move on to the next house regardless.

His new operations manager had warned him that too many bins had been missed on his round, especially on Mondays, and this unprofessional attitude must cease, forthwith.

Joey knew he was on thin ice, so he decided to try a little bit harder to get all the wheelie bins emptied. After what he thought was, a very successful day, he returned to the council depot, to have his work sheet signed off by the new operations manager.

On checking the work sheet, the new operations manager noticed that one pick-up had not been done. It was a new customer, i.e. **the Chinese takeaway**.

Joey tried to explain that he had knocked on the door and shouted through the letterbox but there was no reply from the takeaway. He was told in no uncertain terms that he was to return to the takeaway and empty the bin or face disciplinary action!

Joey made his way back to the takeaway like a bat out of hell! On arrival the front door was open and a little Chinese man was mopping the floor. Joey bounced in and shouted: "Hey you!"

Chinese man: "How … how … how you know my name?"

Joey: "Don't be a smart Alec. Where's your BIN!"

Chinese man: "I been CHINA!"

Joey: "I'm not mucking about! Where's your BIN!"

Chinese man: "I been CHINA!"

Joey: "NO! NO! NO! Where's your WHEELIE BIN?"

Chinese man: "AAAYE WEALLY BEEN CHINA!"

* * *

The Chinese takeaway was struggling a little throughout its first three months of business.

Due to Monday, Tuesday and Wednesday nights being fairly quiet, it was decided to put on a few special offers to create a little more custom on those particular nights.

Joey thought he would check it out. When he arrived on Monday night, he was really pleased that the special offers available were his favourites!

Joey: "Can I just check that these prices are OK?"

Chinese Man: "AAAHSO! Chicken flied lice, beef flied lice and plawn flied lice … all half plice! Gleat bargains for you, Misa Binman!"

Joey: "Right then. I'll have an extra large portion of chicken fried rice!"

On Tuesday night Joey ordered an extra large portion of beef fried rice!

On Wednesday night Joey ordered an extra large portion of prawn fried rice!

The following week Joey returned to take advantage of the special offers. When he arrived at the takeaway on the Monday night he once again checked the prices.

Joey: "Can I just check that the prices are still OK?"

Chinese Man: "AAAHSO! Special offers have finished! chicken fried RICE, beef fried RICE and prawn fried RICE all normal price."

Joey: "Last week you said lice, not RICE!"

Chinese Man: "Last week we had no RICE! Just special offers!"

* * *

Wee Bruce arrived as a newborn but unfortunately he arrived with nothing below the neck! All he had was his head. Over the years that followed he didn't grow much but he developed a great sense of humour. Well, it was a case of having to!

On the night of his 18th birthday his dad planned something different for him.

Dad: "Well son, you don't get to be 18 every day so, I've got a special surprise for you."

Bruce: "Not another feckin' hat!"

Dad: "No son."

Bruce: "I don't need another pair of feckin' sunglasses!"

Dad: "No, son."

Bruce: "Well then! What have you got me?"

Dad: "Well son. I'm going to introduce you to alcohol! Yes, I'm taking you down to the pub for a night out!"

Bruce: "That's sounds great to me. Let's go!"

Anyway, Dad put his coat on and wrapped a wee scarf around Bruce's wee head. As it was raining Dad put the hood of his coat up and slipped Bruce into a bag for life from **Tesco** to keep his wee head dry and off they dandered down the road to the pub.

Dad was swinging the plastic bag to and fro, whistling happy birthday and Bruce could be heard joining in from within!

When they arrived at the pub, Dad produced Bruce from the bag and the party began almost immediately! Best wishes and good luck from everyone there, with the odd wise crack about not being able to shake Bruce's hand or pat him on the back!

After about three hours or so the party was definitely in full swing. Everyone and anyone, were all well oiled, especially Dad and Bruce! Dad decided he needed to go to the toilet so he made sure that Bruce's head was steady on the bar and slurred: "I'm goin' for a well-deserved pish. You stay here until I get back … and … and … don't go anywhere … and … and … don't get into any trouble! OK!

Bruce: "OK DA!!! DO ONE FOR ME!!! HEE! HEE! HEE!"

When Dad returned to the bar there were broken tables and chairs and glasses all over the floor and Bruce was rolling back and forward along the bar with his head cut open, a broken nose and scratches to his face!

Dad: "What the f**k happened son?"

Bruce: "When you were in the toilet a big fight started and someone shouted …

STICK THE F****N' HEAD IN!"

* * *

The teacher at primary school promised her class of seven-year-olds that anyone who could make up a little poem could leave for home at half past two instead of three o'clock!

One little boy puts his hand up and said: "Miss, I know one."

Teacher: "Well then, what are you waiting for?"

Little boy: "My name is Dan. When I grow up to be a man, I want to marry a girl from China, or Japan!"

Teacher: "Well done Daniel! You can leave at half past two. Now, anyone else?"

A little girl puts her hand up and says: "Miss, I know one."

Teacher: "Off you go then!"

Little girl: "My name is Mary Brady. When I grow up to be a lady, I want to have a baby!"

Teacher: "Well done Mary. You can leave at half past two. Now, anyone else?"

Another little boy puts his hand up and says: "Miss, I know one."

Teacher: "OK. Off you go!"

Little boy: "My name is also Dan. When I grow up to be a man, f**k that bird in China or Japan! If Mary Brady wants her baby, I'm her fecking man!"

* * *

The following day the teacher decides to test the class on their times tables!

First up is a little boy at the front of the class. He is asked to recite the five times table.

Little Boy: "Five ones are five. Five twos are ten. Five trees are fifteen. Five fours are twenty. Five fives are twenty five, and so on up to five times ten."

Teacher: "Very well done!"

The second pupil was a little girl. She was asked to recite the six times table.

Little Girl: "Six ones are six. Six twos are twelve. Six threes are eighteen. Six fours are twenty four. Six fives are thirty, and so on up to six times ten."

Teacher: "Excellent!"

The third pupil is wee Sammy. He is asked to recite the seven times table.

Wee Sammy: "Nah nah nah nah. Nah nah nah nah. Nah nah nah nah."

Teacher: "Hang on a minute Sammy. What do you think you are doing?"

Wee Sammy: "Well Miss, I know how it goes. I just forgot the words!"

* * *

After his second term as Prime Minister, David Cameron is to be knighted!

On arrival at Buckingham Palace, he makes his way to the ceremonial chamber and kneels down in front of HM The Queen to receive his well-deserved award.

The Queen taps him gently on each shoulder with the ceremonial sword and says: "Arise Sir David!"

David Cameron remains perfectly still.

Once again the Queen taps him gently on each shoulder and says: "Arise Sir David!"

David Cameron remains perfectly still.

The Queen is becoming a little irate so, on the third occasion she taps him strongly on each shoulder and SHOUTS: "ARISE SIR DAVID!"

A voice from behind the Queen says: "Tell him to get up! He wouldn't know what a bloody rise was!"

* * *

A hare was running across a road in a small country village. Unfortunately it was run over by a car driven by a passing tourist. The driver, who was a middle-aged man, stopped the car and quickly got out to see what it was he had, in fact, run over.

A little old lady who lived nearby and had witnessed the accident also surveyed the scene of the unfortunate dead hare and the unfortunate distressed driver! The little old lady said: "Hang on a minute son. I have something indoors that will rectify the situation!"

She returned as quick as a flash with a plastic bottle in her hand. She removed the top of the plastic bottle and sprinkled some of the contents over the dead hare.

After only a few seconds, the hare came alive and jumped up on to its paws, looked left and right and then scarpered through a hole in a nearby hedge! He then ran like the clappers through a large open grassy field.

He then stopped, turned to face the little old lady and the driver and gave a gentle wave with his right, front paw!

After another three or four yards, he stopped again and gave another gentle wave. This time continued until he was over a faraway hill and out of sight.

The driver turned to the little old lady and said: "That's an absolute miracle. What did you sprinkle over the hare?"

The little old lady replied: "Hair restorer …with a very light permanent wave!"

* * *

The local council offices in Enniskillen were in need of a facelift. A lick of paint, a few repairs here and there and a general all round clean-up.

A local councillor named Alex was tasked to out-source the task in hand and in turn came up with what he thought was a suitable shortlist.

There were three small companies on the list and a rep from each one was invited to Alex's office to discuss terms.

The first man to come in was from Belfast:

Alex: "How much will you charge to carry out the work?"

Belfast man: "£3,000 is the best I can do."

Alex: "Can you break that down for me?"

Belfast man: "Of course I can. £1,000 for materials, £1,000 for labour, £1,000 for profit."

Alex sends him out and asks the second one to come in, who was from Dublin.

Alex: "How much will you charge to carry out the work?"

Dublin man: "£6,000 is the best that I can do."

Alex: "Can you break that down for me?"

Dublin man: "Of course I can. £2,000 for materials, £2,000 for labour, £2,000 for profit."

Alex sends him out and asks the third one to come in, who was from Cork.

Alex: "How much will you charge to carry out the work?"

Cork man: "£9,000 is the best I can do."

Alex: "That's a bit steep. Can you break it down for me?"

Cork man: "Of course I can. £3,000 for you, £3,000 for me, and we'll get the Belfast man to do the job!"

* * *

A barrister from London was on a business trip to Belfast. As he was driving around Belfast in his top of the range Mercedes Benz, the bus lanes and the one way system had him totally confused!

On checking his classy Rolex wrist watch, he realised that if he didn't get a move on, he was going to be late for his most important meeting of the day.

As he approached a T-junction leading on to the main road that he recognised would lead him to his destination, he noticed a traffic sign that read **STOP.**

He slowed down slightly, looked to his right, saw no oncoming traffic and continued the motion by gently pulling away with a smile of satisfaction on his face, as he would now be sure he would be on time for his very important appointment.

From out of nowhere appeared a police patrol car! The police officer signalled for the Merc to pull over. As he did so the barrister lowered the driver's side window and demanded to know why he was stopped.

Barrister: "Why have I been stopped? I am on my way to a very important appointment!"

Policeman: "Well now sir. I'm afraid you are guilty of a traffic violation."

Barrister: "Explain yourself my man!"

Policeman: "When you came to the T-junction back there you failed to stop."

Barrister: "But there was no traffic coming from my right, therefore I slowed down and then I proceeded on my merry way!"

Policeman: "Oh really?"

Barrister: "Yes! Oh really!"

Policeman: "The sign clearly says STOP. And that means STOP."

Barrister: "Look my good man! I am a qualified barrister from London and I can assure you that I know what I'm talking about. I know the law! I didn't have to stop as long as I slow down before turning onto the main road!"

Policeman: "Oh Really! STOP means STOP … not slow down! You are bound by the law of the road to STOP and not just SLOW DOWN! Do you understand me?"

Barrister: "My good man. You must listen to me!"

Policeman: "I am not, nor will I ever be your good man! Now get out of the friggin' car!"

Barrister: "Well, I never!"

With that the policeman dragged the London barrister out of the Merc and frog marched him behind a nearby hedge. He withdrew his cosh from his belt and began to beat the living daylights out of the barrister's head!

Barrister: "Stop! Stop! Please stop!"

Policeman: "Do want me to STOP … or just SLOW DOWN!"

* * *

During an election campaign the usual callers were making their rounds, drumming up votes from the local community.

One particular pensioner was sick and tired of the usual false promises. so that he would barely give the time of day to any of them. He was determined to put all callers on the spot with one simple question: "If I vote for you, how will you look after me?"

The first caller was from the Labour Party.

Pensioner: "If I vote for you, how will you look after me?"

Caller: "We will look after you … from the cradle to the grave!"

The second caller was from the Conservative Party.

Pensioner: "If I vote for you, how will you look after me?"

Caller: "We will look after you … from the womb to the tomb!

The third caller was from UKIP.

Pensioner: "If I vote for you, how will you look after me?"

UKIP: "We will look after you … from the erection to the resurrection!"

* * *

A young Irish lad was travelling on the train from Liverpool to London. He soon made his way to the buffet car for a few beers.

After about 15 minutes another young lad arrived with the same thought in mind. The young Irish lad recognised the new customer's Welsh accent.

Irish Lad: "Hello there. Are you from Wales?"

Welsh Lad: "Yes I am."

Irish Lad: "Well then, what's your name?"

Welsh Lad: "I was born on St David's Day so my mam, well, she called me David."

A short time later another young lad arrived and soon all three were enjoying a good old drink and a good old chinwag! The new arrival had a strong Scottish accent.

Irish Lad: "Hey there mate, what's your name?"

Scottish Lad: "I was born on St Andrew's Day and my maw insisted on calling me Andy."

A third young lad joined their company a few minutes later and immediately the young Irish lad offered him a drink. The new arrival had a soft English accent.

Irish Lad: "Come and join us. Oh by the way, what's your name?"

English Lad: "I was born on St George's Day and my mum, guess what, she called me Georgie. By the way mate, what's your name?"

Irish Lad: "Pa … Pa … Pancake!"

* * *

The Irish and Welsh pig farmers were taking part in a European Directive, whereby they would take it in turn to visit each other's pig farms to compare and share their local knowledge regarding breeding techniques.

Paddy arrived at Dai's pig farm late in the afternoon and they both agreed that the best way to get to know each other was to go down to the only pub in the village for a few drinks.

A few developed into a lot, and a lot developed into a bin-full At about ten o'clock that night they were making their way back slowly but surely, linking arms so as not to fall over, through the village to Dai's pig farm.

Just outside the village there was a church. There was an unusual grunting sound coming from the area of the churchyard. On further investigation the two farmers were astounded to see one of Dai's pigs, which had escaped from the farm, with its head wedged into a gap in the metal railings surrounding the churchyard.

The two drunken men staggered closer to the poor pig, which was now in a complete panic, twisting and turning, trying to free itself, with its arse wiggling like blazes.

Di: "Right mate, just you follow me."

Paddy: "Hiccup!"

Di begins to unzip his trousers and search for his manhood.

Di: "I'll … take my … love hose … out and give … my pig a good blast … right up the F*****G arse!"

Paddy: "Hiccup!"

When Di had done the dirty deed he stood back and said:

"Right Paddy! Now it's your turn!"

Once again Paddy replied: "Hiccup!"

Paddy swayed towards the stricken pig, dropped his trousers and then stuck his own head … **into the railings!**

* * *

Tommy-Joe got himself a job as a deckhand on a submarine, when it was announced over the loud speaker to … **DIVE! DIVE! DIVE!**

Tommy-Joe dived in. It was ten days later when he was picked up by a fishing boat. At his disciplinary hearing he was asked by the judge: "Why did you desert your post?"

Tommy-Joe: "It came over the loud speaker to DIVE! DIVE! DIVE! So I DIVED IN! And it's a good thing I did DIVE IN!"

Judge: "Why's that?"

Tommy-Joe: "The F*****G thing SANK!"

* * *

A man was at home watching the football on the TV on a Saturday afternoon. His wife had gone out shopping and asked him to keep an eye on their 16-year-old daughter.

At half-time the 16-year-old daughter, was complaining that she was bored watching the football! She moaned, moaned, moaned, until her dad got so fed up he gave her £2 to go to the corner shop, owned by his uncle, to buy some sweets!

After the match the dad realised that his daughter had not returned. Panic stricken, he shot out the door and down to the corner shop. On going inside he found the small shop to be empty, but he could hear moaning and groaning from behind the door leading into the living area!

He opened the door! And there was his 16-year-old daughter, on the sofa, flat on her back, her knickers around her ankles and the uncle, with his head buried between her thighs!

The dad beat the daylights out of the uncle and had him arrested! The girl's mother could not bear to attend the court hearing but insisted that her husband did! When he came home his wife asked: "He must have been found guilty! What sentence did he get?"

Husband: "He got off with it!"

Wife: "How come?"

Husband: "He had a LICKER LICENCE!"

* * *

An American tourist was travelling on a train through the highlands of Donegal. It was known as the Donegal Express. When the train got to a very, very steep hill the conductor made the following announcement:

"First class passengers stay where you are!

"Second class passengers get off and walk!

"Third class passengers get off and push!"

The **Yank** complained how this so-called Donegal Express was slower than slow and then made the following remark: "Back in the States we have bicycles that go faster than this!"

The conductor ignored him completely.

A short time later the train approached a very sharp bend and slowed down almost to a walking pace, and the **Yank** made the following remark: "Back in the States the bends are so sharp that the driver can shake hands with the conductor at the back!"

To which the conductor replied: "Over here the bends are so sharp that the driver can see the back of his FECKIN' NECK!"

* * *

The British Government decided to hold a referendum regarding changing from the **pound** to the **Euro.**

It was agreed that a trial mini referendum would take place in West Belfast. They were simply asked: "How do you feel about changing to the Euro?"

99 per cent said: "Och ney! We'd rather just stick with the GIRO!"

Why did the Republic of Ireland change to the Euro?

Because PUNT rhymed with bank manager.

* * *

Big Leo was an apprentice at the local undertakers when Mrs Murphy's body was brought in for burial. Bendy Benny, the head man, laid her out on the table and told Big Leo to keep an eye on things until he came back from the chippy with their lunch.

When Bendy Benny returned Big Leo whispered: "Hey Bendy Benny! Mrs Murphy's got a prawn between her legs."

Bendy Benny: "That's not a prawn you eejit, it's a clitoris!"

Big Leo: "Well now, it tastes like one!"

* * *

Wee Dennis who was a Belfast boy, was only 17 when he left home for work in London. On arrival his uncle Sammy got him a start on a local building site in Camden Town, quite close to their digs.

On the first day, when the workforce settled down for their lunch break, wee Dennis noticed that his uncle Sammy produced a long round container from his rucksack. Uncle Sammy unscrewed the top, which had a small handle on it, rested the top on the table and, of course, wee Dennis could see it was indeed a small cup!

Uncle Sammy unscrewed a smaller inner top and, to wee Dennis' complete wonderment, poured what appeared to be some hot tea from the container into the small cup!

Well f***k me! Wee Dennis sat in absolute wonderment as he had never seen anything like it before!

Wee Dennis: "Uncle Sammy! Uncle Sammy! What's that machine called?"

Uncle Sammy: “Well now son. This thing here, it’s called a vacuum flask. It can keep things warm or, it can keep things cool. It depends what you put in it.”

Wee Dennis: “Can I get one of those vacuum things to bring to work tomorrow?”

Uncle Sammy: “Of course you can son. We’ll pick one up tonight on the way back to the digs and you can bring it to work tomorrow and, sure, you can show everyone that you are one of the boys.”

The following day, wee Dennis showed up at work with his brand new vacuum flask in his rucksack. He could hardly wait for lunch hour to show off his new bit of kit! Lunch hour finally arrived and Wee Dennis produced his brand new vacuum flask. He was as pleased as punch.

Uncle Sammy: “I see you’ve got your brand new vacuum flask with you today.”

Wee Dennis: Ooooh yeees!

Uncle Sammy: “What have you got in it son?”

Wee Dennis: “Three cups of tea … and a choc ice!”

* * *

MICK WIT

(If you can't laugh at yourself)

1. He who walks with a **limp!** Runs with a **hop!** But you can't notice it when he's sittin' **down!**

2. A dog is for **Christmas**. Not just for **life**.

3. Who said: "I am six foot two in me socks?"
   LONGFELLOW.

4. What new name was suggested for Belfast after the Good Friday Agreement?
   LUTON TOWN.

5. If Boris Johnston could fly … **BACON** would go up!

6. I wouldn't say the woman next door was ugly, but she has a **FACE** my dog wouldn't lick!

7. Are you **readin'** that paper you're **sittin'** on?

8. What's the difference between a **DICKHEAD** and a **WANKER**?
   A DICKHEAD tries very hard, but in most cases, fails miserably.
   A WANKER doesn't try at all.

9. What do you call four dogs and a blackbird?
   THE SPICEGIRLS.

10. What are three things you rarely see in Belfast?
A Chinese bin man!
A black man walkin' a dog!
A council worker workin'!

11. If you want to run with the big dogs: **Don't** piss like a poodle.

12. Better to light a candle than wake up with a **DOG** in the morning!

13. What's black and white and red all over? A pregnant **NUN** in confession!

14. If you'd known you were goin' to live so **long,** you'd have looked after yerself **better!**

15. Half of the married people in Belfast are **women** and half the lies they tell aren't **true.**

16. You're like your **mother's brother's** people, you neither work nor want and **hell** will never be filled till you're in it!

17. After two more shots of **poteen,** you'll not remember yourself tomorrow.

18. When speaking in public, always remember the first three and last three letters of the alphabet:
ABC … Always Be Cheerful!
XYZ … Xamine Your Zip!

19. Versions of Lady Chatterley's Lover:
German version = **Hans Felthercrack**
Russian version = **Nibble Hertitsoff**
Irish version 1st edition = **She was only a milkman's daughter but she knew every inch of his root!**
Irish version 2nd edition = **She was only a pilot's daughter but she kept her cockpit clean!**

20. What is the definition of an Irish housewife?
A deaf and dumb nymphomaniac with an off licence.
PS: **With a pool table!**
PPS: **With a dart board!**

21. Why do brides like to get married in white?
Because it matches the colour of all the kitchen appliances!

22. Why do women have small feet?
So they can stand closer to the sink!

23. What is the definition of the Irish chastity belt?
Clunk click! No dick!

24. Why is a snooker table green?
If you'd that many balls and six holes you'd be green too!

25. My spouse:
Take my wife! **Somebody please … take my F******G wife!**
She ran off with my next door neighbour. **I was ever so upset. I missed him terribly!**
She has everything a man wants. **Broad shoulders! Hairy chest! Spare razor blades!**

26. Did you hear about the **Irish Rock n Roll band?**
One Two Five Seven o'clock rock!

27. Did you hear about the **Irish punk rocker?**
He pierced his eyeballs!
He carried a flick hammer!

28. Did you hear about the horny shepherd?
He kept mountain goats!

29. Did you hear about the horny undertaker?
He was in dead earnest!

30. Did you hear about the horny cowboy?
He rode into town and shot up the sheriff!

31. Did you hear about the Irish sea scout?
His tent sunk!

32. What has an Irish submarine and a used condom got in common?
They are both full of thick seamen!

33. What's white and glides across the floor?
Come dancing!

34. Why does the Pope wear underpants in the shower?
He doesn't like looking down at the unemployed!
PS: His phone number is **VAT 19!**

35. Irish dog trials:
Five found guilty but all received suspended sentences!

36. What's the most famous Irish fish?
Sardines – How many blokes do you know who can squeeze themselves into a room of that size, lock the door and put the key on the F*****G outside?

37. Irish wife says to Irish husband: **Your dinner's burnt.**
He asks: **Why?**
She says: **The fish and chippy caught fire!**

38. Thinnest books of the year:
The Irish Space Program.
The Jewish Book of Gifts.
The Scottish Free Drinks Brochure.

39. Did you hear about the Irish referee?
He flooded the pitch to bring on a sub!

40. Before Sir Ben Kingsley became a successful actor he was a male model:
FOR GOLF BALLS!

41. GOLF = **Gentlemen Only Ladies Forbidden!**

42. They say sex is great at **40**, but I've also tried it at number **38** and number **42**! Apart from the queues, it's just as good!

43. Give me a sentence that contains the word fascinate:
I have a duffle coat with nine buttons but I can only fasteneight!

44. Give me a sentence that contains the following words:
Defence
Defeat
Detail
The horse jumped over defence, defeat before detail!

45. Why does your mate call you donkey?
EEYAW, EEYAW EEYAWAYS calls me that!

46. How many animals can you get into a girl's pair of tights?
Two little piggies, two calves, an ass, a wee pussy cat and all the hares you want!

47. There are two boiled eggs walking down the street, which one is the female?
The one with the crack!

48. What lies under the table in a brown paper bag at the last supper?
Judas's Carryout!

49. What's the difference between a light on and a hard-on?
You can go to sleep with a light on!

50. In the words of Henry VIII when he first spoke to one of his many wives:
I won't be keeping you long!

51. In the words of the late great Seamus Heaney when he was late for an appointment:
Apologies, I am slightly fragrant!
In my own words:
Apologies I am under the affluence of inkerhol.

52. If the answer to the question is Cock Robin. What is the question?
    What's that up me arse, Batman?

53. What has Batman and a Scouser got in common?
    They can never go out without Robbin.

54. Potential suspects in Liverpool:
    Bin Fightin'
    Bin Drinkin'
    Bin Thievin'
    But no one can find … Bin workin'

55. I want to die just like my grandfather! Out like a light!
    Not like his screaming passengers!

56. Why have Italian men got big hairy moustaches?
    So they can look more like their mothers!

57. Why did you drive your lorry over that old lady who was lying in the middle of the road?
    I thought she was dead your honour!

58. How many MPs does it take to change a light bulb?
    Two! One to pour the gin and tonics and one to phone the electrician!

59. Wife said to husband: **The doctor said that I have a pretty fanny!**
    Husband said to wife: **No he didn't! He said that you had acute angina!**

60. Did you hear about the Irish man who thought that Muffin the Mule was …
A sex offence.

61. What do you call an Irish electrician?
Shaundaleer!

62. What do you call an Irish window cleaner?
Paddy O' Doors!

63. Did you hear about the Irish man who tried to hang himself with an elastic band?
He died of concussion!

64. Did you hear about the Irish man who was struck by lightning?
He thought he was having his photograph taken!

65. Did you hear about the Irish man who bought his wife a microwave bed?
She can now get eight hours sleep in three minutes!

66. Did you hear about the Irish man who was a member of the secret seven?
It was that secret, he didn't know who the other six were!

67. Paddy and his missus went to a wife swapping party.
He couldn't get the colour television or the pool table!

68. Did you hear about the dyslexic alcoholic?
He choked on his own Vimto!

69. What's the difference between an Irish wedding and an Irish funeral?
    There's one less drunk at the funeral!

70. May the hairs on your arse turn into drumsticks and beat the **f***k** out of you!